cute clothes for kids

Over **35** items to make for
0–5 year olds

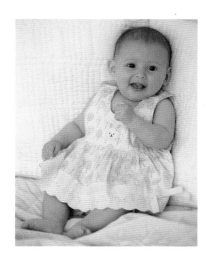

ROB MERRETT

CICO BOOKS

LONDON NEW YORK

DEDICATION

To Luis, Maru, and Mishka

ACKNOWLEDGMENTS

First, a big thank you to CICO Books for another very special opportunity. In particular, to Cindy Richards for nurturing the initial idea, Pete Jorgensen for calmly organizing text, sketches, patterns, and prototypes, and Sally Powell for sourcing models and locations.

Thank you also to Sarah Hoggett for her support, enthusiasm, and keen editorial eye, Christine Wood for her inspiring design and layout, and Kate Simunek for her exceptional illustrations.

Finally, a huge and very special thank you to Terry Benson, whose energy and enthusiasm never fail to inspire.

This book was a great opportunity to work with some wonderful kids, so a special THANK YOU and BIG HUG to all my adorable pint-sized models: Amelie C and Amelie H, Ben, Blu, Ebraheem, Eva, Harry, Imani, Nina, Noah, River, Sophie, and Willow.

Published in 2011 by CICO Books
An imprint of Ryland Peters & Small Ltd
20–21 Jockey's Fields 519 Broadway, 5th Floor
London WC1R 4BW New York, NY 10012

www.cicobooks.com

10 9 8 7 6 5 4 3

Text © Rob Merrett 2011
Design and photography © CICO Books 2011

A CIP catalog record for this book is available from the Library of Congress and the British Library.

ISBN 978 1 907563 83 6

Printed in China

Editor: Sarah Hoggett
Designer: Christine Wood
Illustrator: Kate Simunek
Pattern and template illustrator:
  Stephen Dew
Photographer: Terry Benson
Art direction and styling:
  Rob Merrett

CONTENTS

Introduction

More and more, today's consumer values things that are properly and honestly made. In a world of cheap, sweatshop mass production, fancy merchandizing, and sometimes misleading advertising, this little book will show you just how easy it is to produce practical and contemporary children's clothes involving one of the most traditional crafts. Each sewing project is guaranteed to bring individual style to your little one's wardrobe without costing the earth.

This book is not simply about making clothes, however; it's about making clothes that are different, clothes that are more inspiring than what most stores have to offer. Take time out to enjoy the process of making something with your own hands and experience the sense of pride and satisfaction that are very much a part of the end result.

Always be on the lookout for novel and imaginative trims—check out your local fabric and notions store. Or why not recycle? Remnant fabrics, faded table linens, and soft furnishings can be stitched into new items, giving your sewing projects a unique richness and reassuring sense of familiarity. Cute buttons, embroideries, and ribbons from worn-out wardrobe favorites can also be saved for one-off embellishments.

My aim is to dress children as children—unfortunately, these days they're not little for very long—in clothes that will take them effortlessly from one occasion to another, clothes that are ideal for everyday wear and special days throughout the year. The projects are designed to offer lots of choice. For girls there are fairytale party frocks, strappy sundresses, and a chic little coat; for boys, there are no-fuss pull-on pants, cool beach shirts, and streetwise hoodies.

I hope to encourage the idea of crafting and sewing, and can guarantee plenty of creative fun along the way. However, don't forget the importance of good-quality materials, equipment, and patience—craft with care and the payback will be immense.

Happy sewing... remembering to pin and baste (tack) first!

Tweetie Pie

This dainty sundress is devoid of fussy "girlie" detailing, yet extremely feminine—a perfect example of the "less is more" diktat. It's easy to make and, if you're short of time, lengths of pretty ribbon can replace the dainty shoulder ties. The charming birdcage print in fresh, acidic colors, together with the flounced "petticoat-effect" lining, suggest a totally carefree spirit.

You will need

* Pattern C—front (C1), back (C2), and shoulder tie (C3)

* 20 in. (50 cm) print fabric, 44 in. (112 cm) wide

* 10 in. (25 cm) lining fabric, 44 in. (112 cm) wide

* Matching thread

SIZE: 3, 6, AND 9 MONTHS

Take 3/8-in. (1-cm) seam allowances throughout, unless otherwise stated.

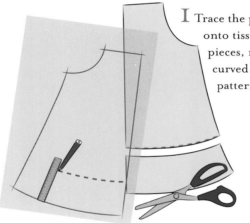

I Trace the pattern pieces you need from the pull-out sheets onto tissue paper. Before cutting out the dress pattern pieces, measure 5 in. (12.5 cm) up from the bottom curved edges and redraw the curves. Cut out the paper pattern along the redrawn lines.

2 Using the new pattern pieces, cut one front, one back, and eight shoulder ties in the print fabric. Cut two 3³/₈ x 27¹/₂-in. (8.5 x 70-cm) and two 5³/₄ x 27¹/₂-in. (14.5 x 70-cm) strips for the flounces in the print fabric. Cut one front and one back in the lining fabric. Transfer all pattern markings onto the fabric before removing the paper pattern pieces.

3 Make the shoulder ties (see page 113). Turn right side out, press, and put to one side.

4 Pin and machine stitch the narrow strips of fabric right sides together to form a loop. Press open the seams. Double hem one long edge (see page 113), turning over ¹/₄ in. (5 mm) and then ³/₈ in. (1 cm) to the wrong side. Repeat with the wide strips.

5 With right sides together, machine stitch the front and back of the dress together at the side seams. Press the seams open. Repeat to make the dress lining.

6 Gather both loops from step 4 into flounces the same width as the bottom of the dress (see page 114). With right sides together, attach the outer (narrow) flounce to the bottom edge of the dress, making sure the gathers are evenly spaced. Baste (tack) in place and then machine stitch. Attach the right side of the inner (wide) flounce to the wrong side of the bottom of the dress lining, again making sure that the gathers are evenly spaced. Baste (tack) and machine in place.

7 With right sides together, aligning the raw edges, pin a shoulder tie to each top corner of the front and back "bib" areas of the dress, ⅜ in. (1 cm) in from the edge of the armhole. Secure with a few machine stitches.

8 With right sides together, pin the dress to the lining, matching the side seams and aligning all edges. Machine stitch all the way around the armholes and front and back "bib" areas. Carefully trim away the seam allowances, snip the corners, and clip the curved edges.

9 Turn the dress right side out, bag out the "bib" areas, turn the ties upward, and carefully press the finished edges of the front and back bodice areas.

10 To finish, knot the ties together to form shoulder straps.

Little Monster

This gruesome twosome is easy-peasy to make, especially as one of the items has already been made for you. The store-bought T-shirt is customized with a playful motif that reflects the whimsical print of the micro shorts. This is a simple process if you decide to apply the motif with a hot iron only; however, although it's a little fiddly, you will achieve a more professional look and secure finish if you edge the motif with a small, dense zigzag stitch or hand-sewn blanket stitch.

You will need

FOR THE T-SHIRT

* Store-bought T-shirt
* Appliqué motifs 1–2 on page 122
* Scraps of cotton poplin/sheeting in assorted colors
* Fusible bonding web
* Matching or contrasting thread

FOR THE SHORTS

* Pattern B—front/back shorts (B1)
* Pocket template 2 on page 125
* 12 in. (30 cm) print fabric, 44 in. (112 cm) wide
* 18 in. (46 cm) bias binding, 1 in. (24 mm) wide
* 1½ in. (4 cm) contrast bias binding, ¾ in. (20 mm) wide
* 15 in. (38 cm) elastic, ½ in. (13 mm) wide
* Matching thread

SIZE: 3, **6**, AND 9 MONTHS

Take ⅜-in. (1-cm) seam allowances throughout, unless otherwise stated.

1 Trace the skull and bone motifs onto thin card and cut out. Cut squares of fusible bonding web large enough to accommodate the motifs. Lay the squares on the wrong side of your appliqué fabrics, adhesive side down, and press with a hot iron to heat bond.

2 Place the card templates on the paper-backed side of their respective appliqué fabrics and draw around them with a pencil. Carefully cut out the motifs (one skull and two bones) and put them to one side.

3 Decide on the position of the motifs and apply them to the front of the garment (see page 118). Using a small zigzag stitch, sew all the way around the motifs. Start with the skull, then do the eye socket and nostril, and finish with the crossbones.

1 Trace the pattern pieces you need from the pull-out section onto tissue paper and cut out. Cut two front/back sections and two 6-in. (15-cm) squares for the patch pockets in print fabric. Transfer all pattern markings onto the fabric before removing the paper pattern pieces.

2 Bind the top edge of each pocket square with a 6-in. (15-cm) length of bias binding (see page 118). Complete the patch pockets (see page 117).

3 To make the pocket loops, fold the remaining bias binding in half lengthwise and topstitch as close as possible along both edges. Cut the strip in half, fold each piece into a loop as illustrated, and machine stitch to secure the folds.

4 Lay a pocket on top of one leg, 2³⁄₈ in. (6 cm) up from the bottom raw edge and 3¹⁄₂ in. (9 cm) in from the center front raw edge. Insert a loop beneath the bottom edge of the pocket and a folded 1¹⁄₂-in. (4-cm) strip of contrast binding into the side for the pocket tab, and topstitch close to the edges of the pocket. Repeat for the second leg.

5 With right sides facing and aligning the raw edges, fold the back section of the shorts onto the front. Pin, baste (tack), and machine stitch the inner leg seam. Repeat for the other leg. Press open the seams.

6 Turn one leg right side out and pull it into the other leg so that the right sides are facing. With raw edges aligned, pin, baste (tack), and machine stitch along the entire curved center seam from the front top edge to the back top edge. Trim the seam allowance and snip the curves.

7 Make a casing for the elasticated waistband (see page 116). Thread the elastic through the casing, adjusting it to fit the waist comfortably. Sew the ends together and stitch the opening closed.

8 Double hem the shorts (see page 113), turning the bottom edge over to the wrong side by ¹⁄₄ in. (5 mm) and then again by ³⁄₈ in. (1 cm).

Picnic

Perfect for the beach or a summer picnic, this simple, practical playsuit is a breeze to make. Honest-to-goodness gingham checks give it a delightful, freshly laundered appeal, while contrasting buttons and tabs at the side seam and pocket edges add novelty and color interest.

You will need

* Pattern A—front bodice (A1), front leg (A2), back bodice (A3), back leg (A4), and front pocket (A5)

* Pocket template 1 on page 125

* Martingale template on page 124

* 32 in. (80 cm) gingham fabric, 44 in. (112 cm) wide

* Three 1½-in. (4-cm) strips of bias binding, ¾ in. (20 mm) wide

* Five ¾-in. (20-mm) buttons

* Lightweight fusible interfacing

* Matching thread

SIZE: **3**, 6, AND 9 MONTHS

Take ⅜-in. (1-cm) seam allowances throughout, unless otherwise stated.

1 Trace the pattern pieces you need from the pull-out sheets onto tissue paper and cut out. Cut two front and two back bodices in the gingham fabric, placing the straight (center back/center front) edges of the pattern pieces on the folded edge of the fabric. Cut two front legs, two back legs, and two front pockets from folded gingham fabric. Cut three 4¾-in. (12-cm) squares and a 4¾ x 6¼-in. (12 x 16-cm) rectangle for the martingale from the remnants. Transfer all pattern markings onto the fabric before removing the paper pattern pieces.

2 Reinforce the shoulder strap areas of one front and one back bodice piece with lightweight fusible interfacing (see page 112); these pieces will form the bodice lining.

3 With right sides together, machine stitch the front and back bodice together at the side seams. Press the seams open. Repeat with the bodice lining pieces.

4 As a folding guide, machine stitch ⅜ in. (1 cm) up from the bottom cut edges of the bodice lining. Following the stitch line, carefully fold under the seam allowances and press.

5 With right sides together, pin the lining to the bodice, matching the side seams. Machine stitch all the way around the armholes, shoulder straps, and necklines. Carefully trim away the seam allowances, snip the corners, and clip the curved edges.

6 Turn the lining to the inside, bag out the shoulder straps, and press. Topstitch the pressed edges of the bodice.

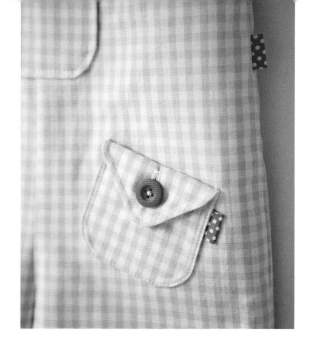

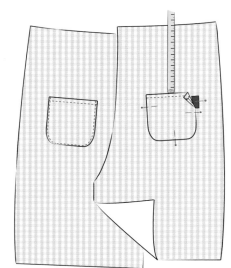

7 Make three patch pockets from the 4¾-in. (12-cm) squares (see page 117) and put one aside for later. Attach two of the pockets to the back legs, about 5 in. (12.5 cm) down from the top raw edge and 2 in. (5 cm) in from the center back raw edge, inserting a folded 1½-in. (4-cm) strip of bias binding into the side of one pocket for the pocket tab.

8 Make the two-piece front pocket (see page 117). Topstitch around the front pocket and make a buttonhole in the triangular-shaped end for the flap. Fold over the flap and press. Sew a button to the pocket to correspond with the buttonhole when the flap is folded over.

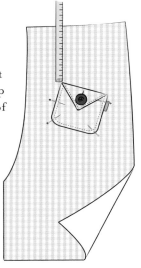

9 Pin the pocket to the front leg at an angle, 4 in. (10 cm) from the top raw edge, and insert a folded strip of bias binding into the side for the pocket tab. Topstitch around the sides and lower edge of the pocket.

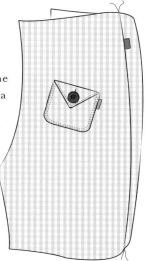

10 With right sides together, lay the front legs on the back legs and insert a folded 1½-in. (4-cm) strip of bias binding into the side seam of one leg for the side tab. Machine stitch the side seams together. Press the seams open.

11 With right sides together, fold the front legs onto the back legs and machine stitch the inner leg seams together. Press the seams open. Turn one leg right side out and pull it into the other leg, so that the right sides are facing. With raw edges aligned, pin, baste (tack), and machine stitch along the entire curved center seam from the front top edge to the back top edge. Trim the seam allowance and snip the curves.

I2 With right sides together and matching the side seams, machine stitch the bottom front and back edges of the bodice to the top front and back edges of the pants. Press the seam allowances toward the bodice.

I3 Line up the folded and pre-stitched bottom edge of the bodice lining with the seam between the bodice and the pants. Pin and slipstitch in place, passing the needle under the stitches so that they meet edge to edge for a neat, flat finish.

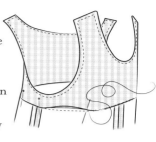

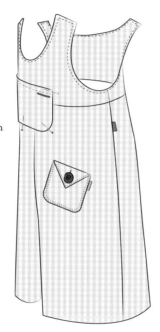

I4 Make a buttonhole in the remaining patch pocket, using a contrasting color of thread. Pin the pocket to the front of the playsuit, midway between the bodice and pant sections. Topstitch along the sides and lower edge of the pocket.

I5 Make a buttonhole in each of the front shoulder straps, starting ⅝ in. (1.5 cm) in from the top edge. Sew a button to each of the back shoulder straps.

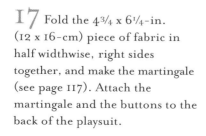

I6 Double hem the pants (see page 113), turning the bottom edge over to the wrong side by ¼ in. (5 mm) and then again by ⅜ in. (1 cm).

I7 Fold the 4¾ x 6¼-in. (12 x 16-cm) piece of fabric in half widthwise, right sides together, and make the martingale (see page 117). Attach the martingale and the buttons to the back of the playsuit.

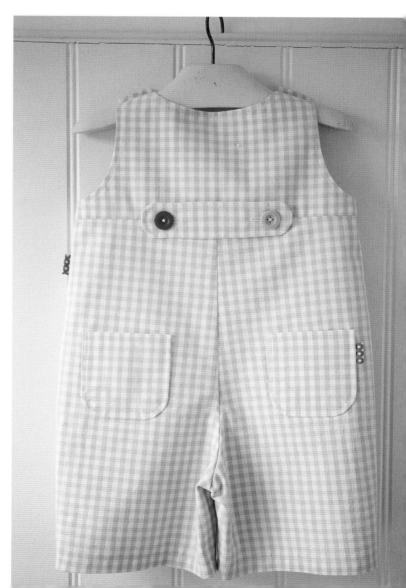

Millefiori

This no-nonsense playsuit is transformed into something extra special with the help of an enchanting millefiori—simply translated as "thousand flowers"—printed cotton fabric and vintage crocheted lace trim. A cute tailored bow provides the finishing touch to this mini showstopper.

You will need

* Pattern A—front bodice (A1), front leg (A2), back bodice (A3), and back leg (A4)
* 40 in. (100 cm) print fabric, 44 in. (112 cm) wide
* Lightweight fusible interfacing
* 100 in. (250 cm) crocheted lace trim, 1 in. (25 mm) wide
* Two ³/₄-in. (20-mm) buttons
* Matching thread

SIZE: 3, 6, AND 9 MONTHS

Take ³/₈-in. (1-cm) seam allowances throughout, unless otherwise stated.

I Trace the pattern pieces you need from the pull-out sheets onto tissue paper and cut out. Cut two front bodices and two back bodices in the print fabric, placing the straight (center back/center front) edges of the pattern pieces on the folded edge of the fabric. Cut two front legs, two back legs, and two 5 x 24½-in. (12.5 x 62-cm) strips for the flounces in the print fabric. Transfer all pattern markings onto the fabric before removing the paper pattern pieces.

2 Reinforce the shoulder-strap areas of the front and back bodice linings with fusible interfacing (see page 112).

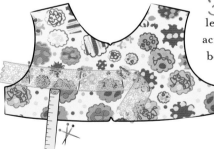

3 Pin and baste (tack) a length of crocheted lace across the front of one front bodice section, 1½ in. (4 cm) up from the bottom cut edge. Zigzag stitch the lace in place.

4 With right sides together, machine stitch the front bodice to the back bodice at the side seams. Press the seams open.

5 Repeat step 4 to make the bodice lining. As a folding guide, machine stitch ³/₈ in. (1 cm) up from the bottom cut edges of the bodice lining. Following the stitching line guide, fold under the seam allowances and press.

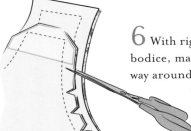

6 With right sides together, pin the lining to the bodice, matching the side seams. Machine stitch all the way around the armholes, shoulder straps, and necklines. Carefully trim the seam allowances, snip the corners, and clip the curved edges.

7 Turn the lining to the inside, bag out the shoulder straps, and press. Topstitch around the armholes and neckline.

8 With right sides together, lay the left pants front on the left pants back and machine stitch the side seams together. Press the seams open. Double hem the leg (see page 113), turning the bottom edge over to the wrong side by ¼ in. (5 mm) and then again by ⅜ in. (1 cm). Pin and baste (tack) a length of crocheted lace along and above the hem, so that the top edge of the lace meets the topstitching. Zigzag stitch the lace in place. Repeat for the right leg.

9 With right sides together, fold each front pants section onto the back pants section and machine stitch the inner leg seams together. Press the seams open. Turn one leg right side out and pull it into the other leg so that the right sides are facing. Aligning the raw edges, pin, baste (tack), and machine stitch along the entire curved center seam from the front top edge to the back top edge. Trim the seam allowance and snip the curves.

10 Machine stitch the two strips of fabric together along the short edges to form a loop. Press open the seams. Double hem the loop along the bottom edge (see page 113), turning it over to the wrong side by ¼ in. (5 mm) and again by ⅜ in. (1 cm). Pin and baste (tack) a length of crocheted lace along and above the hem, so that the top edge of the lace meets the topstitching. Zigzag stitch the lace in place and finish the join in the trim.

11 Gather the loop into a flounce the same width as the bottom of the bodice (see page 114). Attach the flounce to the top edge of the pants section, making sure that the gathers are evenly spaced all the way around. Baste (tack) and then machine stitch the flounce in place.

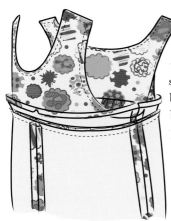

12 With right sides together and matching the side seams, machine stitch the bottom edges of the outer bodice to the top edges of the pants. Press the seam allowances toward the bodice.

13 Line up the folded and pre-stitched bottom edge of the bodice lining with the seam between the bodice and pants. Pin and slipstitch in place, passing the needle under the stitches so that they meet edge to edge for a neat, flat finish.

14 Make a buttonhole in each of the front shoulder straps, starting about ⅝ in. (1.5 cm) down from top edge. Sew a button to each of the back shoulder straps.

15 Make a tailored bow for the front bodice from an 8-in. (20-cm) length of crocheted lace trim (see page 118). Lay the bow on top of the crocheted lace trim across the center of the bodice and stitch it in place.

You will need

FOR THE DRESS

* *Pattern A—front bodice (A1) and back bodice (A3)*
* *24 in. (60 cm) print fabric, 44 in. (112 cm) wide*
* *50 in. (125 cm) eyelet trim (broderie anglaise), 2³⁄₈ in. (6 cm) wide*
* *63 in. (160 cm) bias binding, ¹⁄₂ in. (13 mm) wide*
* *Iron-on animal appliqués*
* *Lightweight fusible interfacing*
* *Two ³⁄₄-in. (18-mm) buttons*
* *Matching thread*

FOR THE PANTIES

* *Pattern B—front/back (B1)*
* *10 in. (25 cm) print fabric, 36 in. (90 cm) wide*
* *19 in. (48 cm) bias binding, ¹⁄₂ in. (13 mm) wide*
* *Iron-on animal appliqués*
* *32 in. (80 cm) elastic, ¹⁄₄ in. (5 mm) wide*
* *Matching thread*

SIZE: **3**, 6, AND 9 MONTHS

Take ³⁄₈-in. (1-cm) seam allowances throughout, unless otherwise stated.

Spring Orchard

Sugared almond-hued and ultra-feminine, this charming day dress and panties set will delight both young and young-at-heart. Made in a cotton printed with dainty sapling motifs and detailed with pretty scalloped hemline, cute tailored bow, and sweet-natured appliqués, this is a cracking spring outfit for an Easter egg hunt.

TO MAKE THE DRESS

I Trace the pattern pieces you need from the pull-out sheets onto tissue paper and cut out. Cut two front bodices and two back bodices in the print fabric, placing the straight (center back/center front) edges of the pattern pieces on the folded edge of the fabric. Cut two 6³⁄₄ x 24¹⁄₂-in. (17 x 62-cm) strips for the front and back skirt in the print fabric. Transfer all pattern markings onto the fabric before removing the paper pattern pieces.

2 Reinforce the shoulder strap areas of one front and one back bodice piece with lightweight fusible interfacing (see page 112); these pieces will form the bodice lining.

3 With right sides together, machine stitch the outer front and back bodices together at the side seams. Press the seams open. Repeat for the bodice lining.

4 As a folding guide, machine stitch ³⁄₈ in. (1 cm) in from the bottom cut edges of the bodice lining. Following the stitch line, carefully fold under the seam allowances and press.

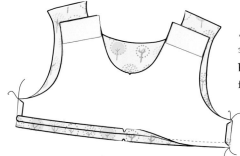

5 With right sides together, pin the lining to the bodice, matching the side seams. Machine stitch all the way around the armholes, shoulder straps, and necklines. Trim away the seam allowances, snip the corners, and clip the curved edges.

6 Turn the lining to the inside, bag out the shoulder straps, and press. Topstitch the pressed edges of the bodice.

7 To make the skirt, machine stitch together the two 6¾ x 24½-in. (17 x 62-cm) strips of fabric to form a loop. Press open the seams. Double hem the loop along the bottom edge (see page 113), turning it over to the wrong side by ¼ in. (5 mm) and then again by ⅜ in. (1 cm).

8 Pin, baste (tack), and machine stitch the eyelet trim (broderie anglaise) along the hem of the skirt, neatly finishing the join in the trim at one of the side seams. Repeat with a length of bias binding, placing it on top of the eyelet trim (broderie anglaise), ¼ in. (5 mm) below the top edge.

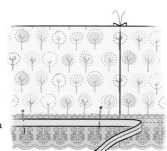

9 Gather the skirt to the same width as the bottom of the bodice (see page 114). Attach the skirt to the bottom edge of the bodice, matching the side seams and making sure the gathers are evenly spaced all the way around. Baste (tack) and machine stitch in place.

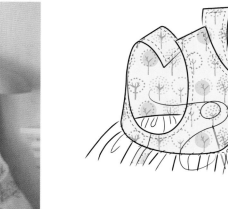

10 Line up the folded and pre-stitched bottom edge of the bodice lining with the seam between the bodice and the skirt. Pin and slipstitch in place, passing the needle under the stitches so that they meet edge to edge for a neat, flat finish.

11 Make a buttonhole in each of the front shoulder straps, starting ⅝ in. (1.5 cm) in from the top edge. Sew a button to each of the back shoulder straps.

12 Following the manufacturer's instructions, apply the iron-on animal motifs to the center front bodice.

1 Trace the pattern from the pull-out sheets onto tissue paper. Before cutting out, shorten the bottom of the legs by 2 in. (5 cm). Cut out the new pattern piece along the redrawn line. Cut out one left and one right leg in the print fabric.

2 Stitch a length of bias binding down the center of each leg to create a side stripe.

3 Fold over ⅜ in. (1 cm) to the wrong side along the bottom of the legs, press, and finish with picot edging (see page 118).

4 Ruffle the legs of the panties (see page 114).

5 With right sides facing and aligning the raw edges, fold the back of one leg onto the front. Pin, baste (tack), and machine stitch the inner leg seam. Repeat for the other leg. Press open the seams.

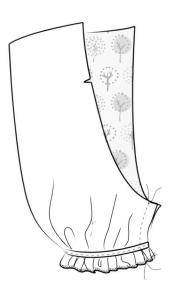

6 Turn one leg right side out and pull it into the other leg, so that the right sides are facing. With raw edges aligned, pin, baste (tack), and machine stitch along the entire curved center seam from the front top edge to the back top edge. Trim the seam allowance and snip the curves.

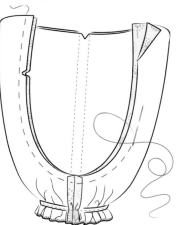

7 Make a casing for the elastic waistband (see page 116), folding over ¼ in. (5 mm) and then ¾ in. (2 cm) of the top edge to the wrong side. Thread elastic through the casing, adjusting it to fit the waist comfortably. Sew the ends together and stitch the opening closed.

8 Following the manufacturer's instructions, apply the iron-on animal motif to one leg of the panties, close to the side stripe.

* *Pattern C—front (C1), back (C2), and shoulder tie (C3)*
* *Pocket template 1 on page 125*
* *Pocket template 3 on page 125*
* *20 in. (50 cm) main fabric, 44 in. (112 cm) wide*
* *20 in. (50 cm) contrast fabric, 44 in. (112 cm) wide*
* *Scrap of plain cotton fabric for flower center*
* *Scrap of fusible bonding web*
* *44 in. (110 cm) bias binding, ¾ in. (2 cm) wide*
* *Matching thread*

FOR THE PANTIES

* *Pattern B—front/back (B1)*
* *10 in. (25 cm) print fabric, 44 in. (112 cm) wide*
* *32 in. (80 cm) elastic, ¼ in. (5 mm) wide*
* *Matching thread*

SIZE: 3, 6, AND **9** MONTHS

Take ⅜-in. (1-cm) seam allowances throughout, unless otherwise stated.

Double-crosser

Being two-faced can have its good points, especially if it's a little dress made up in two fabrics—basically, two looks in one. How novel and convenient is that? A pair of panties in coordinating fabric provides fun contrast, though you could make a matching pair if you prefer.

TO MAKE THE DRESS

1 Trace the pattern pieces you need from the pull-out sheets onto tissue paper and cut out. Cut one front, one back, four shoulder ties, and two 4¾-in. (12-cm) squares in the main fabric. Cut one front, one back, four shoulder ties, and one 5½ x 11-in. (14 x 28-cm) rectangle in the contrast fabric. Transfer all pattern markings onto the fabric before removing the paper pattern pieces.

2 With right sides together and aligning the raw edges, make the shoulder ties (see page 113), using one main fabric and one contrast fabric tie in each pair.

3 Fold the 5½ x 11-in. (14 x 28-cm) piece of contrast fabric for the flower pocket in half lengthwise, right sides together. Place the flower pocket template on top and draw around it. Pin the layers together and machine stitch along the drawn lines, leaving a gap in the stitching at the bottom edges to turn the pocket right side out. Remove the pins, cut around the edges leaving a narrow seam allowance, and cut small wedges between the corners of the petals.

4 Carefully turn the pocket right side out, neaten the bottom edge by tucking in the seam allowance, and press. To make the flower center, take a scrap of plain cotton fabric and back it with fusible bonding web (see page 112). Cut out a circle and apply it to the center of the flower (see page 118). Topstitch along the top edge of the pocket, as illustrated.

5 Approximately 6 in. (15 cm) in from the side seam, machine stitch a 3-in. (8-cm) length of unfolded bias binding to the main fabric dress front to create a flower stalk. Place the flower pocket over the stalk and stitch in place, leaving the top section of the pocket open.

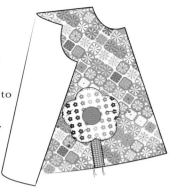

6 Make two patch pockets from the 4¾-in. (12-cm) squares (see page 117). Machine stitch the pockets to the contrast fabric dress front approximately 2⅜ in. (6 cm) in from the side seam and 3½ in. (9 cm) up from the bottom edge.

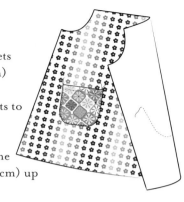

7 With right sides and matching print facing and raw edges aligned, pin a shoulder tie to each top corner of the front and back main fabric dress, ⅜ in. (1 cm) in from the edge of the armhole. Secure with a few machine stitches.

8 With right sides facing, machine stitch the main fabric front and back dresses together at the side seams, and press the seams open. Repeat with the contrast fabric front and back dresses.

9 With right sides together, matching the side seams and aligning all edges, pin the main fabric and contrast fabric dresses together. Machine stitch all the way around the armholes and front and back "bib" areas. Carefully trim the seam allowances, snip the corners, and clip the curved edges.

10 Turn the dress right side out, bag out the "bib" areas, turn the ties upward, and press the finished edges of the front and back bodice areas. Topstitch close to the outer edges.

11 Smooth the double-layered dress so that it's free of wrinkles, match the side seams, and pin the layers together at the bottom edges. Machine stitch the layers together ⅝ in. (1.5 cm) from the bottom raw edge and carefully trim away the seam allowances close to the outside edge of the stitching.

12 Bind the bottom edge of the dress in one continuous action (see page 118), leaving about 2⅜ in. (6 cm) of binding unstitched at each end. Join the ends of the bias binding, insert the unbound section of hem into it, and close with machine stitches.

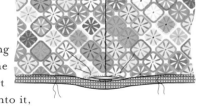

13 To finish, knot the ties together to form shoulder straps.

1 Trace the pattern from the pull-out sheets onto tissue paper. Before cutting out, shorten by 2 in. (5 cm). Cut out the new pattern piece along the redrawn line.

2 Fold over the bottom of the legs to the wrong side by ³/₈ in. (1 cm), press, and finish with picot edging (see page 118).

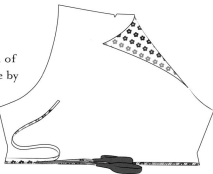

3 Ruffle the legs of the panties (see page 114).

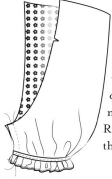

4 With right sides facing and aligning the raw edges, fold the back of one leg onto the front. Pin, baste (tack), and machine stitch the inner leg seam. Repeat for the other leg. Press open the seams.

5 Turn one leg right side out and pull it into the other leg, so that the right sides are facing. With raw edges aligned, pin, baste (tack), and machine stitch along the entire curved center seam from the front top edge to the back top edge. Trim the seam allowance and snip the curves.

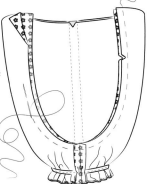
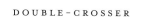

6 Make a casing for the elastic waistband (see page 116), folding over ¹/₄ in. (5 mm) and then ³/₄ in. (2 cm) to the wrong side. Thread elastic through the casing, adjusting it to fit the waist comfortably. Sew the ends of the elastic together and hand stitch the opening closed.

Skateboard Buddies

Designed for the pint-sized "ripper," this terrific two-piece is totally "off the hook" and guaranteed to turn heads as your little one attempts to carve up the suburban landscape. The pants are easy to make; the T-shirt even more so, as it's store bought and customized—a great way of transforming a generic, nondescript, and mass-market item into a stylish one-off. Customization is also a great way of breathing new life into a well-loved item that desperately needs updating when your kids' clothing budget is tight.

You will need

FOR THE T-SHIRT

* Store-bought T-shirt
* Appliqué motif 1 on page 124
* Scraps of cotton poplin/sheeting in black and two contrasting colors
* Fusible bonding web
* Matching or contrasting thread

FOR THE PANTS

* Pattern E—front/back (E1)
* Pocket template 4 on page 125
* Pocket flap template 5 on page 125
* 27 in. (68 cm) checked fabric, 44 in. (112 cm) wide
* 24 in. (60 cm) bias binding, ³/₄ in. (20 mm) wide
* 1¹/₂ in. (4 cm) contrast bias binding, ³/₄ in. (20 mm) wide
* Four ³/₄-in. (20-mm) buttons
* Lightweight fusible interfacing
* 15 in. (40 cm) elastic, ¹/₂ in. (13 mm) wide
* Matching thread

SIZE: 3, 6 AND 9 MONTHS

Take ³/₈-in. (1-cm) seam allowances throughout, unless otherwise stated.

TO MAKE THE T-SHIRT

1 Cut four squares of fusible bonding web large enough to accommodate the motif. Lay the squares on the wrong side of the appliqué fabrics, adhesive side down, and press with a hot iron to heat bond; you will need two black pieces and one in each contrasting color.

2 Trace the entire skateboard motif onto thin card and cut out. Place the template on the paper-backed side of the black appliqué fabric and draw around it twice with a pencil. Carefully cut out the motifs.

3 Decide on the position of the motifs and attach them to the front of the garment (see page 118).

4 Cut the wheels off the card template and discard. Place the board template on the paper-backed side of the contrasting fabrics and draw around it with a pencil. Cut out the motifs and apply on top of the black skateboards.

5 Using a small zigzag stitch, sew all the way around the motifs, starting with the board and then the wheels.

6 Using a denser zigzag stitch, sew along the entire length of each board. When stitching onto the front and the right side of the motif, it is advisable to turn the T-shirt inside out to avoid accidentally stitching into the back panel of the garment.

SKATEBOARD BUDDIES

1 Trace the pattern pieces you need from the pull-out sections onto tissue paper and cut out. Cut two front and two back pant sections and four 6¾ x 7½-in. (17 x 19-cm) pieces for the flap patch pockets in the checked fabric. Transfer all pattern markings onto the fabric before removing the paper pattern pieces. Back two of the pocket pieces with lightweight fusible interfacing (see page 112).

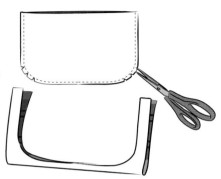

2 To make a pocket bag, fold under ¾ in. (2 cm) to the wrong side along one edge of one non-interfaced pocket piece. Complete the patch pocket, following the instructions on page 117.

3 Make a pocket flap (see page 117), clip around the curves, and turn right side out. Press, topstitch around the edges, and make two diagonal buttonholes.

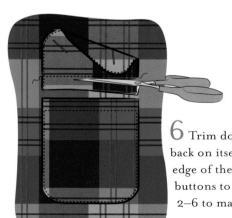

4 Lay a pocket bag on top of one leg, 7 in. (18 cm) down from the raw edge of the waistline. Insert a folded 1½-in. (4-cm) strip of contrast binding into the side for the pocket tab and topstitch close to the edges of the pocket.

5 Place the pocket flap directly above the pocket bag, leaving a ⅜-in. (1-cm) gap in between, and stitch in place.

6 Trim down the seam allowance, fold the flap back on itself, press, and machine stitch the top edge of the flap through all thicknesses. Sew buttons to the pocket bag to finish. Repeat steps 2–6 to make the pocket for the other leg.

7 With right sides together, fold the front section of the pants onto the back section and machine stitch the inner leg seams together. Press the seams open. Repeat for the other leg.

8 Turn one finished leg right side out and pull it into the other finished leg, so that the right sides are facing. With raw edges aligned, pin, baste (tack), and machine stitch along the entire curved center seam from the front top edge to the back top edge. Trim the seam allowance and snip the curves.

9 Make a casing for the elasticated waistband (see page 116). Thread the elastic through the casing, adjusting it to fit the waist comfortably. Sew the ends together and stitch the opening closed.

10 To make the fake drawstring, fold the 24-in. (60-cm) length of bias binding in half widthwise, press the fold, and machine stitch as close as possible along the edge. Fold under and machine stitch the ends of the tie to neaten. Sink stitch the middle of the tie onto the center front waist and tie it in a neat bow.

11 Double hem the pants (see page 113), turning the bottom edge over to the wrong side by ¼ in. (5 mm) and then again by ⅜ in. (1 cm).

Flower Power

This teeny-weeny trapeze top scattered with psychedelic florals in eye-popping hues pays homage to 1960s hippies. The circular shoulder yoke, simple and neat, is trimmed with another '60s throwback—a dainty tailored bow. Roomy pajama pants in soft, springy linen complete the look, with the vivid floral print reappearing for turn-ups and a fake drawstring.

You will need

FOR THE TOP

* Pattern D—front (D1), front yoke (D2), back (D3), and back yoke (D4)

* Pocket template 1 on page 125

* 20 in. (50 cm) print fabric, 44 in. (112 cm) wide

* 30¾ in. (78 cm) bias binding, ⅝ in. (15 mm) wide for hem

* 35 in. (90 cm) bias binding, ¾ in. (20 mm) wide, for armholes, pocket, and bow

* 1½-in. (4-cm) strip of satin ribbon

* 6-in. (15-cm) zipper

* Matching thread

FOR THE PANTS

* Pattern E—front/back (E1)

* 20 in. (50 cm) plain fabric, 44 in. (112 cm) wide

* 8 in. (20 cm) print fabric, 44 in. (112 cm) wide

* 15 in. (40 cm) elastic, ½ in. (13 mm) wide

* Matching thread

SIZE: 3, 6, AND 9 MONTHS

Take ⅜-in. (1-cm) seam allowances throughout, unless otherwise stated.

TO MAKE THE TOP

1 Trace the pattern pieces you need from the pull-out sheets onto tissue paper and cut out. Cut one front (on the folded fabric), two front yokes, two backs, and two back yokes in print fabric. Cut one 4¾-in. (12-cm) square in print fabric for the pocket. Transfer all pattern markings onto the fabric before removing the paper pattern pieces.

2 With right sides together, machine stitch the two back panels to the front panel at the side seams and then press open the seams.

3 Pin and baste (tack) a 12-in. (30-cm) length of bias binding around one armhole and edge stitch the binding in place, following the instructions on page 118. Repeat for the other armhole.

4 Fold under ¾ in. (2 cm) along one edge of the 4¾-in. (12-cm) pocket square. Following the instructions on page 118, attach a length of bias binding to the folded edge. Complete the patch pocket (see page 117).

5 Attach the pocket to the front about 1¼ in. (3 cm) up from the lower raw edge and 1⅜ in. (3.5 cm) in from the center front. Insert a folded 1½-in. (4-cm) strip of satin ribbon into the side of the pocket for the pocket tab.

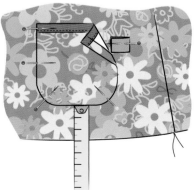

6 With right sides facing, machine stitch the outer front and back yokes together at the shoulder seams and press open the seams. Repeat with the inner front and back yokes. As a folding guide, machine stitch along the outer edges of the inner yoke, 3/8 in. (1 cm) from the edge.

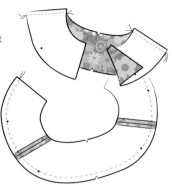

7 With right sides together, pin the outer yoke to the front and back panels of the bodice, matching up the outer edges of the bound armholes with the reference dots on the yoke. Baste (tack) and machine stitch in place.

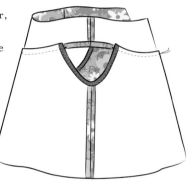

8 Following the stitching line guide, carefully fold under the seam allowance of the inner yoke and press.

9 With right sides together and matching the shoulder seams, pin and baste (tack) the outer yoke to the inner yoke at the neck edge. Machine stitch together and cut out wedges around the curved seam allowance.

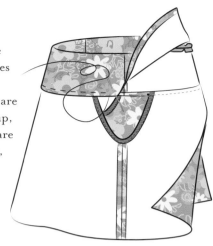

IO Turn the inner yoke over to the inside and carefully match up the edges of both yokes, especially at the armholes. Making sure that the yokes are lying flat, the shoulder seams match up, and the ends of the bound armholes are neatly tucked inside, pin, baste (tack), and edge stitch the entire yoke.

II With right sides facing, taking a 5/8-in. (1.5-cm) seam allowance, machine stitch the back panels together at the center back seam for about 6 in. (15 cm) up from the bottom edge. Make several backstitches to reinforce the seam. Press open the seam and the remaining 5/8-in. (1.5-cm) seam allowances that will form the center back opening.

I2 Place the zipper underneath the center back opening and carefully baste (tack) it in place. Following the basting (tacking) stitches, machine stitch the zipper to the garment through all thicknesses.

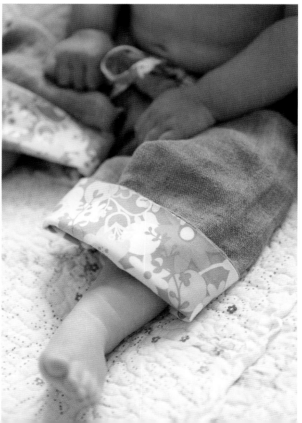

I3 Pin and baste (tack) a 30¾-in. (78-cm) length of bias binding along the entire hem and edge stitch it in place, following the instructions on page 118.

I4 Make a tailored bow (see page 118) for the front shoulder yoke from a 5½-in. (14-cm) length of folded bias binding and attach it to the front yoke.

TO MAKE THE PANTS

1 Trace the lower section of pattern piece E1 from the pull-out sheet onto tissue paper. Measure 4³⁄₄ in. (12 cm) up from the bottom straight edge and draw a horizontal line across the pattern. This is the pattern for the contrast facings on the pant legs.

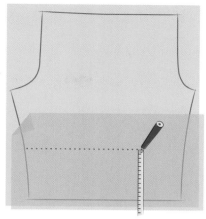

2 Trace the whole of pattern piece E1 from the pull-out sheet onto tissue paper and cut out. Cut two front/back pant sections in plain fabric and two front/back pant facings in print fabric. Transfer all pattern markings onto the fabric before removing the paper pattern pieces.

3 With right sides together, fold the front section of the pants onto the back section and machine stitch the inner leg seams together. Press the seams open. Repeat for the other leg.

4 Fold the pant facings in half widthwise, with right sides facing, and machine stitch the short ends together. Press open the seams. Fold over ³⁄₈ in. (1 cm) of the top edge of both facings to the wrong side and press.

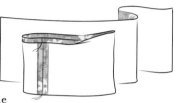

5 Pull the left pant leg into the left facing so that the right sides are together. With the inside leg seams and the bottom edges aligned, pin, baste (tack), and machine stitch the facing to the pant leg, ⁵⁄₈ in. (1.5 cm) up from the bottom edge. Turn the pant leg, with the facing attached, inside out and press open the seam.

6 Turn the facing back onto the wrong side of the pant leg, along the seam, and press the hem seam. Making sure that the layers are lying flat, machine stitch through all thicknesses as close as possible to the folded edge at the top of the facing. Repeat steps 5 and 6 for the right leg.

7 Turn one finished leg right side out and pull it into the other finished leg, so that the right sides are facing. With raw edges aligned, pin, baste (tack), and machine stitch along the entire curved center seam from the front top edge to the back top edge. Trim the seam allowance and snip the curves.

8 Make a casing for the elasticated waistband (see page 116). Thread elastic through the casing, adjusting it to fit the waist comfortably. Sew the ends together and stitch the opening closed.

9 Cut a 1¹⁄₂ x 22-in. (4 x 56-cm) strip from the print fabric and make a fake drawstring (see page 113). Sink stitch the middle of the drawstring onto the top center front waist and tie it in a neat bow.

Spot On

Most little girls dream of owning a *traje de faraleas* ("dress of ruffles"), the flamboyant costume of the Spanish flamenco dancer—so here is a modified, easy-to-wear version. Bold and colorful in style and trimmed with a generous double row of playful flounces, this is a guaranteed showstopper.

You will need

* Pattern F—front (F1) and back (F2)
* Appliqué motif 1 on page 120
* 53 in. (135 cm) print fabric, 44 in. (112 cm) wide
* 5½ x 6½-in. (14 x 16-cm) piece of contrast fabric for appliqué
* 70 in. (170 cm) bias binding, ¾ in. (20 mm) wide
* Lightweight fusible interfacing
* Fusible bonding web
* Two ¾-in. (18-mm) buttons
* Matching thread

SIZE: **1 AND 2 YEARS**

Take ⅜-in. (1-cm) seam allowances throughout, unless otherwise stated.

1 Trace the pattern pieces you need from the pull-out sheets onto tissue paper. Before cutting out the pattern pieces, measure 6½ in. (17 cm) up from the bottom curved edges and redraw the curves. Cut out the paper pattern along the redrawn lines.

2 Using the new pattern pieces cut two fronts, two backs, two 4½ x 31½-in. (11.5 x 80-cm) strips for the two-piece dress flounce, and two 8 x 31½-in. (20.5 x 80-cm) strips for the two-piece lining flounce in the print fabric.

3 Prepare and cut out the appliqué bow motif and apply it to the front of the dress (see page 118).

4 To make the dress flounce, pin the two 4½ x 31½-in. (11.5 x 80-cm) lengths of fabric right sides together and machine stitch the short ends together to form a loop. Press open the seams.

5 Bind the bottom edge of the flounce in one continuous action (see page 118), leaving about 2⅜ in. (6 cm) of bias binding unstitched at each end. Join the ends of the bias binding, insert the unbound section of the flounce into it, and close with machine stitches.

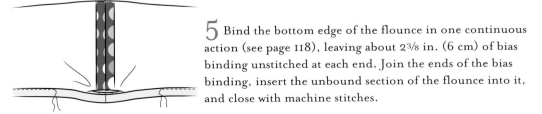

6 Repeat steps 4 and 5 to make the lining flounce with the two 8 x 31½-in. (20.5 x 80-cm) strips of fabric.

7 With right sides facing, machine stitch the two dress panels together at the side seams. Repeat with the two lining panels.

8 Gather the narrow loop into a flounce the same width as the bottom of the dress (see page 114). With right sides together, attach the flounce to the bottom edges of the dress, making sure the gathers are evenly spaced all the way around. Baste (tack) in place and then machine stitch.

9 Gather the wider loop into a flounce the same width as the bottom of the lining (see page 114). Attach the right side of the flounce to the wrong side of the bottom edge of the lining, making sure the gathers are evenly spaced all the way around. Baste (tack) in place and then machine stitch.

10 With right sides together, pin the lining to the dress, matching the side seams. Machine stitch all the way around the back bib, armholes, and shoulder straps. Carefully trim the seam allowances, snip the corners, and clip the curved edges.

11 Turn the lining to the inside, bag out the shoulder straps, and press. Topstitch the pressed edges of the dress.

12 Make a buttonhole in each top corner of the back bib, starting ⅝ in. (1.5 cm) down from the top edge. Sew a button to each shoulder strap.

Hawaiian Tropical

This floral shirt and its coordinating pants would be right at home on the white sands of Waikiki Beach. A dynamic and eclectic mix of vibrant colors, tropical prints, surfing motifs, and active sportswear detailing—what more could a little boy need for his Hawaiian vacation?

TO MAKE THE SHIRT

1 Trace the pattern pieces you need from the pull-out sections onto tissue paper and cut out. Cut two fronts (left and right), one back, two collars, one 4¾-in. (12-cm) square for the pocket, and two 2⅜ x 5-in. (6 x 12.5-cm) pieces for the sleeve tabs in print fabric. Cut two sleeves in plain fabric. Transfer all pattern markings onto the fabric before removing the paper pattern pieces.

2 Stay stitch the necklines ⅜ in. (1 cm) in from the cut edges to prevent them from stretching (see page 112).

3 To make the front facings, lay both front sections wrong side up on your work surface. Turn the center front edges to the wrong side by 1¼ in. (3 cm), press, baste (tack). Turn the front edges to the right side by 1¼ in. (3 cm) and secure with pins. Taking one front section, make a 90° angle at the neck edge by stitching from the folded edge to the dot and up to the upper edge. Trim away the seam allowance and carefully clip into the stitched corner. Turn the front facing right side out and press. Repeat for the other front section.

4 Make five buttonholes in the facing of the left front section, spacing them equally from the top neck to the bottom edge. Put the front sections to one side.

5 Make a patch pocket (see page 117) from the 4³/₄-in. (12-cm) square. Attach the pocket to the left front, inserting the folded 1¹/₂-in. (4-cm) strip of colored tape into the side before stitching to form the pocket tab.

6 Back the appliqué fabric with fusible bonding web (see page 112). Make and apply the appliqué motifs and zigzag stitch around the outline of the surfboards one by one (see page 118).

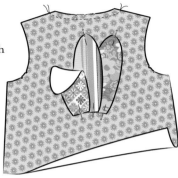

7 Finish the design by applying the letters.

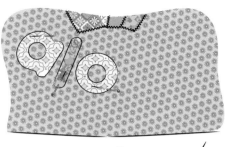

8 With right sides together, machine stitch the front sections to the back at the side and shoulder seams. Press open the seams.

9 Make and attach the collar, following the instructions on page 115.

10 To make the sleeve tabs, fold the 2³/₈ x 5-in. (6 x 13-cm) pieces of print fabric in half widthwise. Machine stitch along the long edge and one short end. Cut around the edges of the sleeve tab, leaving a narrow seam allowance. Turn right side out, press, and make a buttonhole at the finished end.

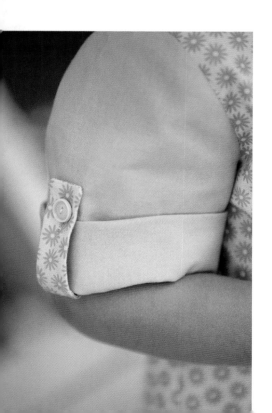

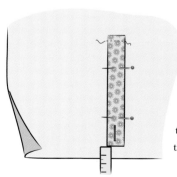

11 Pin a tab to the center of the wrong side of one sleeve, with the buttonhole end lying about 1¹/₂ in. (4 cm) in from the lower raw edge of the sleeve. At the top end of the tab, sew a short row of machine stitches through all thicknesses to secure it in place. Repeat for the other sleeve.

12 Using the longest stitch length, machine stitch ⅜ in. (1 cm) inside and along the top edges of the sleeves between the balance marks, in readiness for easing the sleeves into the armholes.

13 With right sides together, fold the sleeves widthwise, align the raw edges, and stitch the underarm seams. Press open the seams and double hem the sleeves (see page 113), turning the bottom edges over to the wrong side by ¼ in. (5 mm) and again by ⅜ in. (1 cm). Attach the sleeves (see page 114).

14 Double hem the shirt (see page 113), turning the bottom edge over to the wrong side by ¼ in. (5 mm) and then again by ⅜ in. (1 cm).

15 Attach buttons to the front of the shirt and to the sleeves, directly over the row of machine stitches that holds the sleeve tabs in place.

TO MAKE THE PANTS

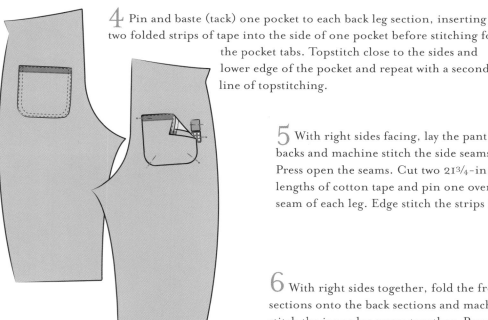

1 Trace the pattern pieces you need from the pull-out sections onto tissue paper and cut out. To make contrast facings for the pant legs, trace the lower section of the front leg pattern H1. Measure 4³/₄ in. (12 cm) up from the bottom straight edge and draw a horizontal line across the pattern at this point. Cut out the front pant facing paper pattern. Repeat for the back pant facing, using pattern H2.

2 Using the new facing patterns together with the existing pattern pieces provided, cut two fronts, two backs, and two 6-in. (15-cm) squares for the pockets squares in the main fabric. Cut two front facings (left and right) and two back facings (left and right) in the contrast floral fabric. Transfer all markings onto the fabric before removing the paper pattern pieces.

3 Fold under ³/₄ in. (2 cm) along one edge of each pocket square. Press in the fold and attach a 6-in. (15-cm) length of cotton tape along the folded edge. Machine stitch in place through all thicknesses, inside both edges of the tape. Complete the patch pockets (see page 117).

4 Pin and baste (tack) one pocket to each back leg section, inserting two folded strips of tape into the side of one pocket before stitching for the pocket tabs. Topstitch close to the sides and lower edge of the pocket and repeat with a second line of topstitching.

5 With right sides facing, lay the pant fronts on the backs and machine stitch the side seams together. Press open the seams. Cut two 21³/₄-in. (55-cm) lengths of cotton tape and pin one over the side seam of each leg. Edge stitch the strips in place.

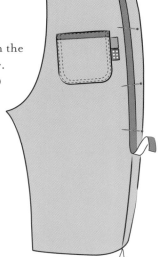

6 With right sides together, fold the front sections onto the back sections and machine stitch the inner leg seams together. Press open the seams.

7 Turn one leg right side out and pull it into the other leg, so that the right sides are facing. With raw edges aligned, pin, baste (tack), and machine stitch along the entire curved center seam from the front top edge to the back top edge. Trim the seam allowance and snip the curves.

8 Fold the pant facings in half widthwise, with right sides facing, and machine stitch the short ends together. Press open the seams. Fold over 3/8 in. (1 cm) of the top edge of both facings to the wrong side and press. Pull the left pant leg into the left facing, right sides together. Aligning the inside leg seams and bottom edges, pin, baste (tack), and machine stitch the facing to the pant leg, 5/8 in. (1.5 cm) up from the bottom edge. Turn the pant leg, with the facing attached, inside out and press open the seam.

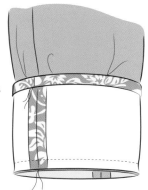

9 Turn the facing back onto the wrong side of the pant leg, along the seam, and press the hem seam. Making sure that the layers are flat, machine stitch through all thicknesses as close as possible to the folded edge at the top of the facing. Repeat steps 8 and 9 for the right leg.

10 Make a casing for the elastic waistband (see page 116). Thread elastic through the casing, adjusting it to fit the waist comfortably. Sew the ends together and hand stitch the opening closed.

11 To make the fake drawstring, fold under the ends of a 22¼-in. (54-cm) length of cotton tape and machine stitch to neaten. Sink stitch the middle of the tape onto the top center front waist seam and tie it in a neat bow.

You will need

* Pattern F—front (F1) and back (F2)
* Pocket template 6 on page 125
* Boat appliqué motifs 1–5 on page 121
* 17 in. (43 cm) light fabric, 44 in. (112 cm) wide
* 9½ in. (24 cm) dark fabric, 44 in. (112 cm) wide
* Two 5½-in. (14-cm) squares of spotted fabric for back pockets
* One 3½ x 6½-in. (8 x 16-cm) piece of white fabric for boat hull appliqué
* Scraps of assorted plain and spotted fabrics for cabin, funnel, and flag appliqués
* 8¾-in. (22-cm) length of grosgrain (petersham) ribbon, ¼ in. (5 mm) wide, for mast
* 13¾-in. (35-cm) length of grosgrain (petersham) ribbon with white stitching, ¼ in. (5 mm) wide, for rigging
* Four 1½-in. (4-cm) strips of spotted bias binding, ¾ in. (20 mm) wide, in assorted colors
* 57 in. (145 cm) bias binding, ½ in. (13 mm) wide
* 6½-in. (16-cm) length of guipure "daisy" trim
* Two ¾-in. (20-mm) buttons
* Five ½-in. (13-mm) buttons
* Fusible bonding web
* Fusible lightweight interfacing
* Matching thread

SIZE: 1 AND **2** YEARS

Take ⅜-in. (1-cm) seam allowances throughout, unless otherwise stated.

Ship Ahoy!

This flattering A-line pinafore will make a trip to the seaside all the more enjoyable for your little ones. Color-blocked panels at front and back provide the ideal backdrop for a jaunty little steamboat, its rigging strung with playful bunting and its funnel spouting a "daisy" smoke plume. The buttons featured here are both functional and decorative, fastening shoulder straps and creating porthole windows that run along the hull. The continuous binding around the neckline and armholes is a little fiddly to attach, but provides the perfect finish.

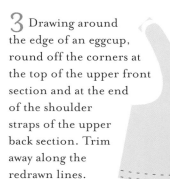

I Trace the pattern pieces you need from the pull-out sheets onto tissue paper. Split both the front and back panels in two by measuring 6¾ in. (17 cm) up from the curved bottom edges and redrawing the curves.

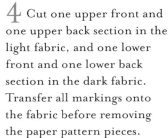

2 Retrace the upper front and back sections and add a ⅜-in. (1-cm) seam allowance to the curved bottom edge. Retrace the lower front and back sections and add a ⅜-in. (1-cm) seam allowance to the curved top edge. Cut out the paper patterns along the redrawn lines.

3 Drawing around the edge of an eggcup, round off the corners at the top of the upper front section and at the end of the shoulder straps of the upper back section. Trim away along the redrawn lines.

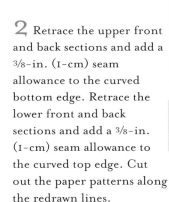

4 Cut one upper front and one upper back section in the light fabric, and one lower front and one lower back section in the dark fabric. Transfer all markings onto the fabric before removing the paper pattern pieces.

5 Lay the upper front section right side up. Pin, baste (tack), and machine stitch the 8¾-in. (22-cm) length of grosgrain (petersham) ribbon to the center front, starting from the lower edge and folding under the end of the ribbon by ⅜ in. (1 cm).

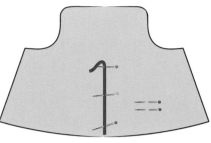

6 Back the appliqué fabrics with fusible bonding web and make the motifs (see page 112). Apply the funnel, then the cabin, and finally the boat hull (see page 118).

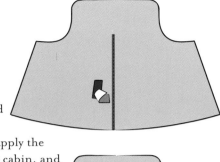

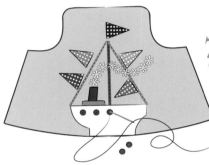

7 To make the rigging, attach the 13¾-in. (35-cm) length of grosgrain (petersham) ribbon with white stitching. Start at the bow of the ship and finish at the stern, folding under each end. Add the flags, "daisy" smoke plume, and "porthole" buttons.

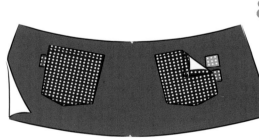

8 Make patch pockets from the 5½-in. (14-cm) squares (see page 117). Attach the pockets to the lower back section 1¼ in. (3 cm) down from the upper raw edge and 4 in. (10 cm) apart, inserting folded 1½-in. (4-cm) strips of bias binding into the sides of the pockets for the tabs.

9 With right sides facing, machine stitch together the upper and lower front sections of the dress. Repeat for the upper and lower back sections of the dress and press the seams open.

10 With right sides facing, machine stitch the dress together at one side seam only, inserting a folded 1½-in. (4-cm) strip of bias binding into the seam on the "horizon" line for the tab. Press the seam open.

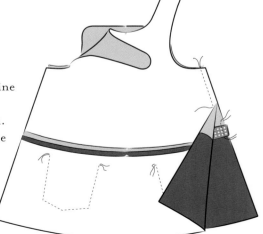

11 Machine stitch around the bib, armholes, and shoulder straps ⅜ in. (1 cm) in from the raw edge, then carefully trim away the seam allowances close to the outside edge of the stitching.

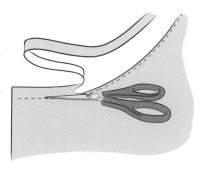

12 Bind the top edges of the dress in one continuous action (see page 118), leaving about 2⅜ in. (6 cm) of binding unstitched at each end.

13 With right sides facing, machine stitch the remaining side seam. Press open the seam. Join the ends of the bias binding, insert the unbound section of armhole into it, and close with machine stitches.

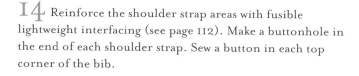

14 Reinforce the shoulder strap areas with fusible lightweight interfacing (see page 112). Make a buttonhole in the end of each shoulder strap. Sew a button in each top corner of the bib.

15 Double hem the dress (see page 113), turning the bottom edge over to the wrong side by ¼ in. (5 mm) and then again by ⅜ in. (1 cm).

You will need

FOR THE TOP

* Pattern F—back (F2)

* Ladybug appliqué motifs 1–3 on page 122

* 12 in. (30 cm) print fabric, 44 in. (112 cm) wide

* 9 in. (23 cm) plain fabric, 44 in. (112 cm) wide

* 32 in. (80 cm) spotted bias binding, ¾ in. (20 mm) wide

* Scraps of red and black fabric for ladybug appliqué

* Five ⅜-in. (10-mm) buttons

* Fusible bonding web

* Matching thread

* Black embroidery floss (thread)

FOR THE PANTS

* Pattern I—front (I1), front yoke (I2), back (I3), and back yoke (I4)

* 18 in. (45 cm) print fabric, 44 in. (112 cm) wide

* 5 in. (12 cm) plain fabric, 44 in. (112 cm) wide

* 17 in. (68 cm) spotted bias binding, ¾ in. (20 mm) wide

* 19 in. (48 cm) elastic, ¼ in. (5 mm) wide

* Matching thread

SIZE: I AND 2 YEARS

Take ⅜-in. (1-cm) seam allowances throughout, unless otherwise stated.

Ladybug

They may be classed as creepy-crawlies, but these enchanting, jewel-like bugs are used here to great effect on a printed two-piece that every budding entomologist will adore. The striking ladybug appliqué that decorates the sun top and mimics the tiny daisy bugs that scurry about below is quick and easy to make. The spotted bindings that accent the bodice are repeated as dainty trims around the hip yoke of the no-fuss, pull-on pants. Light, bright, and breezy, this carefree summertime outfit is the "bee's knees!"

TO MAKE THE TOP

I Trace the pattern piece from the pull-out sheets onto tissue paper. Before cutting out the pattern, measure 1¼ in. (3 cm) up from the top edge and redraw the top line. Measure 1½ in. (4 cm) out from the straight center back edge and redraw the center line.

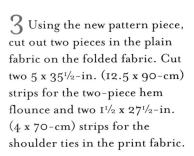

2 Measure 10 in. (25 cm) up from the bottom curved edge and redraw the curve. Cut out the paper pattern along the redrawn lines.

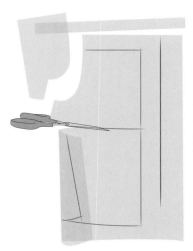

3 Using the new pattern piece, cut out two pieces in the plain fabric on the folded fabric. Cut two 5 x 35½-in. (12.5 x 90-cm) strips for the two-piece hem flounce and two 1½ x 27½-in. (4 x 70-cm) strips for the shoulder ties in the print fabric.

4 To make the appliqué, take the scraps of red and black fabric and, following the manufacturer's instructions, back them with fusible bonding web. Make the motifs, following the instructions on page 112.

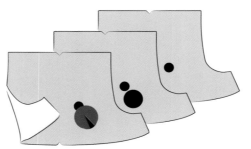

5 Lay the front bodice right side up on your work surface and apply the ladybug's head, body, and wings in sequence, as illustrated.

6 Stitch on black buttons for the ladybug's spots and embroider the antennae in backstitch (see page 119), using black embroidery floss (thread).

7 With right sides facing, machine stitch the front and back bodice together at the side seams and press the seams open. Machine stitch around the armholes 3/8 in. (1 cm) from the raw edge and trim away the seam allowances close to the outside edge of the stitching. Bind each armhole with spotted bias binding (see page 118).

8 With right sides facing, pin and machine stitch the short edges of the two long strips of fabric together to form a loop. Press the seams open. Turn the long bottom edge to the wrong side by 1/4 in. (5 mm) and then again by 3/8 in. (1 cm). Pin, baste (tack), and topstitch as close as possible to the folded edge.

9 Gather the loop to the same width as the bottom of the top (see page 114). With right sides together, attach the loop to the bottom edge of the top, making sure that the gathers are evenly spaced all the way around. Baste (tack), then machine stitch in place.

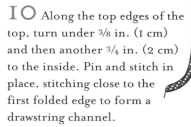

10 Along the top edges of the top, turn under 3/8 in. (1 cm) and then another 3/4 in. (2 cm) to the inside. Pin and stitch in place, stitching close to the first folded edge to form a drawstring channel.

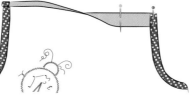

11 Make two shoulder ties from the 1 1/2 x 27 1/2-in. (4 x 70-cm) strips of fabric (see page 113). Using a safety pin, thread one shoulder tie through each channel and tie them together in neat bows.

1 Trace the pattern pieces you need from the pull-out sections onto tissue paper and cut out. Cut two fronts and two backs in print fabric. Cut two front hip yokes (left and right) and two back hip yokes (left and right) in plain fabric.

2 To make the hip yoke trim, open out the 17-in. (68-cm) length of bias binding and press out the creases. Fold it in half widthwise, wrong sides together. Press and cut into four equal-sized strips. With cut edges aligned, lay a length of binding along the top edge of one pant leg. Pin and stitch in place, 1/4 in. (5 mm) in from the edge. Repeat for the other leg sections.

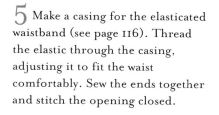

3 With right sides together and aligning the raw edges, pin, baste (tack), and machine stitch the front and back hip yokes to the front and back leg sections. Press the seam allowances toward the yokes. Topstitch the seams close to the edge.

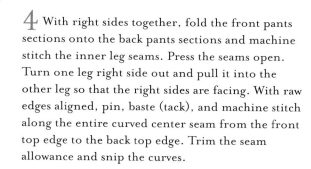

4 With right sides together, fold the front pants sections onto the back pants sections and machine stitch the inner leg seams. Press the seams open. Turn one leg right side out and pull it into the other leg so that the right sides are facing. With raw edges aligned, pin, baste (tack), and machine stitch along the entire curved center seam from the front top edge to the back top edge. Trim the seam allowance and snip the curves.

5 Make a casing for the elasticated waistband (see page 116). Thread the elastic through the casing, adjusting it to fit the waist comfortably. Sew the ends together and stitch the opening closed.

6 Double hem the pants (see page 113), turning the bottom edge over to the wrong side by 1/4 in. (5 mm) and then again by 3/8 in. (1 cm).

You will need

FOR THE SHIRT

* *Pattern G—front (G1), back (G2), and collar (G3)*
* *Pocket template 1 on page 125*
* *Pocket template 6 on page 125*
* *15 in. (40 cm) animal-print fabric, 44 in. (112 cm) wide*
* *5 in. (12.5 cm) plain fabric, 44 in. (112 cm) wide*
* *32 in. (80 cm) bias binding, 5/8 in. (15 mm) wide, for hem and back neck tab*
* *24 in. (60 cm) bias binding, 5/8 in. (15 mm) wide, for armholes*
* *Five 1/2-in. (12-mm) buttons*
* *Fusible lightweight interfacing*
* *Contrast thread*

FOR THE SHORTS

* *Pattern H—front leg (H1), back leg (H2), and pocket (H3)*
* *Pocket template 6 on page 125*
* *15 in. (40 cm) light blue fabric, 44 in. (112 cm) wide*
* *15 in. (40 cm) dark blue fabric, 44 in. (112 cm) wide*
* *12 in. (30 cm) bias binding, 1 in. (25 mm) wide*
* *One 1 1/2-in. (4-cm) strip of bias binding, 3/4 in. (20 mm) wide*
* *Two 1/2-in. (12-mm) buttons*
* *Fusible bonding web*
* *19 in. (48 cm) elastic, 3/4 in. (20 mm) wide*
* *Matching thread*

SIZE: 1 AND 2 YEARS

Take 3/8-in. (1-cm) seam allowances throughout, unless otherwise stated.

Blue Lagoon

This hot, tropical beach combo is totally chilled-out in a refreshing palette of deep sea blues and aquatic greens. Bold jungle fauna animate a traditional, sleeveless shirt, while dynamic color-blocked shorts add fizz to the foam. This summer, get set to make a splash in the surf!

TO MAKE THE SHIRT

1 Trace the pattern pieces you need from the pull-out sections onto tissue paper and cut out. Cut two fronts (left and right), one back, and one 5 1/2-in. (14-cm) square in print fabric. Cut two collars and one 4 3/4-in. (12-cm) square in plain fabric. Transfer all pattern markings onto the fabric before removing the paper pattern pieces.

2 Stay stitch the necklines 3/8 in. (1 cm) in from the cut edges to prevent them from stretching (see page 112).

3 To make the front facings, lay both front sections wrong side up on your work surface. Turn the center front edges to the wrong side by 1 1/4 in. (3 cm), press, and secure with basting (tacking) stitches. Turn the center front edges to the right side by 1 1/4 in. (3 cm) and secure with pins. Taking one front section, make a 90° angle at the neck edge by stitching from the folded edge to the dot and up to the upper edge. Trim away the seam allowance and carefully clip into the stitched corner. Turn the front facing right side out and press. Repeat for the other front section.

4 Make five buttonholes in the facing of the left front section, spacing them equally from the top neck to the bottom edge. Put the front sections to one side.

5 Take the 4¾-in.
(12-cm) and 5½-in. (14-cm)
squares and make patch pockets
(see page 117). Attach each
pocket to its respective
front panel, with the top of
each pocket approximately
7½ in. (19 cm) from the base
of the shirt and centered
widthwise.

6 With right sides together, machine stitch the
front shirt sections to the back shirt section at
the side and shoulder seams. Press the seams open.

7 Make and attach the collar (see page 115).

8 Using the longest stitch length, machine stitch ⅜ in. (1 cm) in from the raw
edges of the armholes. Trim away the seam allowances close to the outside edge
of the stitching and finish each armhole with a 12-in. (30-cm) length of ⅝-in.
(15-mm) bias binding (see page 118).

9 Bind the shirt hem with a 28⅜-in. (72-cm) length of
bias binding in a contrasting color (see page 118).

10 Sew a loop to the
back neck of the shirt as
illustrated, using the
remaining bias
binding, and attach
buttons to the front of
the shirt to finish.

1 Trace the front and back pants patterns from the pull-out sheets onto tissue paper, then draw and cut along the lines that read "cut here for shorts" before pinning the pattern pieces to your fabric. Transfer all pattern markings onto the fabric before removing the paper pattern pieces.

2 Cut two fronts, four pockets, and two 5½-in. (14-cm) squares for the back patch pockets in light blue fabric. Cut two backs in dark blue fabric.

3 Fold under ¾ in. (2 cm) along one edge of each 5½-in. (14-cm) pocket square. Attach a length of bias binding to the folded edge (see page 118). Complete the patch pockets (see page 117).

4 Attach the patch pockets to the back legs about 4 in. (10 cm) in from the upper raw edge. Insert a folded 1½-in. (4-cm) strip of bias binding into the side of one of the pockets for the pocket tab.

5 Take a scrap of print fabric with a suitable animal motif and, following the manufacturer's instructions, back it with fusible bonding web (see page 112). Carefully cut out the motif, lay the right back pants leg right side up on your work surface, and apply the motif (see page 118).

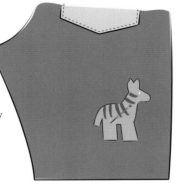

6 Make two two-piece pockets (see page 117). Topstitch along the diagonal edge of the pocket openings, and then across the pockets 2½ in. (6.5 cm) up from the tip of the "flaps." Topstitch around the edges of the pocket "flaps," starting and finishing at the horizontal stitching line. Make a buttonhole toward the lower point of the "flaps."

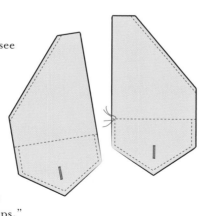

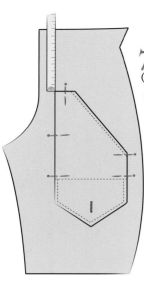

7 Pin each pocket to a front leg, 3½ in. (9 cm) down from the upper raw edge and 1½ in. (4 cm) in from the center front raw edge. Attach the pockets to the legs by topstitching around the edges of the pockets.

8 Sew buttons to the front legs so that they will meet the buttonholes when the triangular flaps are lying flat.

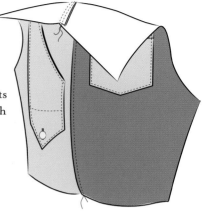

9 With right sides together, lay the pant fronts on the pant backs and machine stitch the side seams. Press the seams toward the pant backs. With the pants sections right side up on your work surface, topstitch through all thicknesses along the side seams.

10 With right sides together, fold the front leg sections onto the back leg sections and machine stitch the inner leg seams together. Press the seams open.

11 Turn one leg right side out and pull it into the other leg so that the right sides are facing. With raw edges aligned, pin, baste (tack), and machine stitch along the entire curved center seam from the front top edge to the back top edge. Trim the seam allowance and snip the curves.

12 Make a casing for the elasticated waistband (see page 116). Thread the elastic through the casing, adjusting it to fit the waist comfortably. Sew the ends together and stitch the opening closed.

13 Double hem the pants (see page 113), turning the bottom edge over to the wrong side by ¼ in. (5 mm) and then again by ⅜ in. (1 cm).

You will need

FOR THE HOODIE

* Pattern J—front (J1), back (J2), and hood (J4)
* Pocket template 7 on page 125
* 20 in. (50 cm) denim fabric, 54 in. (136 cm) wide
* 10 x 15 in. (25 x 38 cm) plain contrast fabric
* 280 in. (200 cm) red bias binding, 1 in. (25 mm) wide
* 70 in. (180 cm) yellow bias binding, 1 in. (25 mm) wide
* 32 in. (80 cm) bias binding, 1 in. (25 mm) wide
* 4 in. (10 cm) decorative tape, 5/8 in. (15 mm) wide
* Two 3/4-in. (20-mm) buttons
* 12-in. (30-cm) open-ended zipper
* Matching thread

FOR THE SHORTS

* Pattern H—front (H1), back (H2), side tab (H4), pocket flap (H5)
* Pocket template 6 on page 125
* 20 in. (50 cm) print fabric, 44 in. (112 cm) wide
* 24 in. (60 cm) bias binding, 1 in. (25 mm) wide
* One 1½-in. (4-cm) strip of bias binding, 1 in. (25 mm) wide
* Three 3/4-in. (18 mm) buttons
* 19 in. (48 cm) elastic, 3/4 in. (20 mm) wide
* Matching thread

SIZE: I AND 2 YEARS

Take 3/8-in. (1-cm) seam allowances throughout, unless otherwise stated.

South of the Border

This two-piece look takes its cue from the great American outdoors—the jeans of the cowboy and the cacti of his stamping ground. The result, however, is quirky and decidedly urban. Denim is used for a street-wise hoodie edged with a bold, sportswear-inspired trim, while a vintage cotton print of potted succulents makes funky, summer-in-the-city shorts.

TO MAKE THE HOODIE

I Trace the pattern pieces you need from the pull-out sections onto tissue paper and cut out. Cut two fronts, one back, two hoods, a 4¾-in. (12-cm) square for the breast patch pocket, and two 7½ x 10-in. (19 x 25-cm) rectangles for the large pockets in the denim fabric. Cut the piece of plain contrast fabric in half to make two 7½ x 10-in. (19 x 25-cm) rectangles for the pocket facings. Transfer all pattern markings onto the fabric before removing the paper pattern pieces.

2 Using one denim rectangle and one plain fabric rectangle for each pocket, make two two-piece pockets (see page 117).

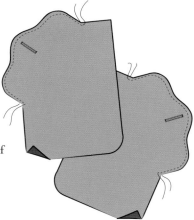

3 Topstitch and buttonhole the flap section of the pockets.

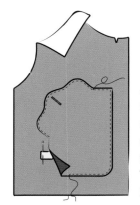

4 Pin one pocket to a jacket front, 1½ in. (4 cm) in from the center front edge and 2 in. (5 cm) up from the lower cut edge, inserting a 2-in. (5-cm) folded strip of decorative tape into the side for the pocket tab before stitching. Topstitch close to the sides and lower edge. Repeat for the other pocket, omitting the tab.

5 Make the breast patch pocket (see page 117). Pin the pocket to the jacket front, 2 in. (5 cm) in from the center front edge and 5/8 in. (1.5 cm) above the large pocket, inserting a 2-in. (5-cm) folded strip of decorative tape into the side for the tab before stitching.

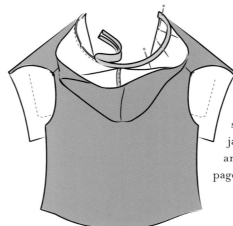

6 Lay the hood sections right sides together and pin and baste (tack). With raw edges aligned, pin an opened-out length of yellow bias binding to the hood. Machine stitch through all thicknesses, trim the seam allowance of the hood, wrap the binding over it, and machine stitch closed.

7 With right sides together, machine stitch the front sections to the back section at the shoulder seams.

8 With right sides facing, machine stitch the hood to the neck edge of the jacket, matching the notches and center seam of the hood with the shoulder seams and center back of the jacket. Trim the curved seam allowance and bind with yellow bias binding (see page 118).

9 With right sides facing and raw edges aligned, lay the jacket front on the jacket back. Machine stitch the side seams and press open the seams.

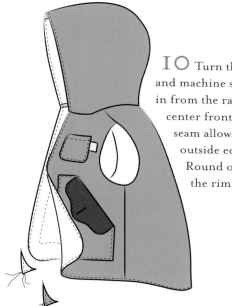

10 Turn the jacket right side out and machine stitch ⅝ in. (1.5 cm) in from the raw edges of the hood, center front, and hem. Trim the seam allowances close to the outside edges of the stitching. Round off the corners, using the rim of a teacup.

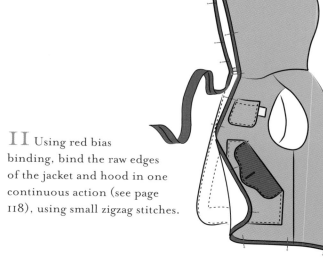

11 Using red bias binding, bind the raw edges of the jacket and hood in one continuous action (see page 118), using small zigzag stitches.

12 Machine stitch ⅜ in. (1 cm) in from the raw edges of the armholes. Trim away the seam allowances close to the outside edge of the stitching and bind each armhole with yellow bias binding, using small zigzag stitches.

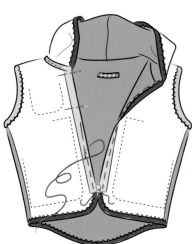

13 Pin and baste (tack) the zipper to the underneath of the jacket front and machine stitch it in place.

14 Sew a button to the pocket so that it will meet the buttonhole when the flap is lying flat and repeat for the other pocket. Fold the remaining yellow bias binding in half widthwise, press, and machine stitch along both edges. Fold under the ends of the strip and machine stitch to the back neck.

1 Trace the pattern pieces you need from the pull-out sections onto tissue paper, drawing and cutting along the lines that read "cut here for shorts." Transfer all pattern markings onto the fabric before removing the paper pattern pieces.

2 Cut two fronts, two backs, four pocket flaps, two side tabs, and two 5½-in. (14-cm) squares for the back pockets.

3 Make two patch pockets for the backs of the shorts (see page 117). Attach the pockets to the back legs about 4 in. (10 cm) down from the upper raw edge, inserting a folded 1½-in. (4-cm) strip of bias binding into the side of one of the pockets for the tab.

4 To make a front pocket flap, place two flap pieces right sides together and carefully sew around the edges, leaving the top straight edge open in order to turn the flap right side out. Remove the pins and carefully cut around the edges, leaving a narrow seam allowance.

5 Carefully turn the flap right side out and press. Topstitch along the edges and ⅜ in. (1 cm) in from the top edge, through all thicknesses. This stitching line will act as a guideline when attaching the flap to the front leg section. Tie the thread ends securely and wrap under. Make a buttonhole toward the lower point of the flap.

6 With right sides facing, pin the pocket flap diagonally across the top of the front leg, as illustrated. Matching the ends of the stitched guideline with the dots marked on the leg section, attach the flap by re-stitching along the guideline through all thicknesses. Make several backstitches to reinforce the ends of the flap. Remove the pins and trim the seam allowance to ⅛ in. (3 mm).

7 Fold the flap back on itself and press. Stitch along the top edge of the flap, through all thicknesses. Sew a button to the front leg so that it will meet the buttonhole when the pocket flap is lying flat. Repeat steps 5–7 to make and attach the other front flap.

8 Place two tab pieces right sides together and sew around the edges, leaving the narrow, straight end open. Remove the pins, carefully cut around the edges leaving a narrow seam allowance, and turn right side out. Topstitch along the edges and make a buttonhole at the pointed end. Aligning the raw edges, place the tab at the outside edge of a leg section, about 5½ in. (14 cm) up from the hem. Secure with a few machine stitches.

9 With right sides together, lay the pant fronts on the pant backs. Machine stitch the side seams and press the seams open.

10 With right sides together, fold the front sections onto the back sections and machine stitch the inner leg seams together. Press the seams open.

11 Turn one leg right side out and pull it into the other leg, so that the right sides are facing. With raw edges aligned, pin, baste (tack), and machine stitch along the entire curved center seam, from the front top edge to the back top edge. Trim the seam allowance and snip the curves.

12 Make a casing for the elasticated waistband (see page 116), folding the top edge over to the wrong side by ⅜ in. (1 cm) and then by 1 in. (2.5 cm), and press. Thread elastic through the casing, adjusting it to fit the waist comfortably. Sew the ends together and stitch the opening closed.

13 To make the fake drawstring, fold the bias binding in half widthwise, press the fold, and machine stitch as close as possible along the edge. Fold under and machine stitch the ends of the tie to neaten. Sink stitch the middle of the tie onto the center front waist and tie it in a neat bow.

14 Double hem the pants (see page 113), turning the bottom edge over to the wrong side by ¼ in. (5 mm) and then again by ⅜ in. (1 cm).

Bits and Bows

This chic little blouse has a dramatic bow tie at the waist that can be worn at the front or the back—and if that wasn't enough to create an air of utter femininity, there are pretty pouffed sleeves that gather gently around the elbow. The simple A-line skirt features a charming floral grouping that mimics the pyrotechnic patterns of the blouse. Use tightly woven cotton poplins for the petals, as this will minimize fraying during washing and wear.

You will need

FOR THE BLOUSE

* *Pattern G—front (G1), back (G2), collar (G3), and sleeve (G5)*
* *36 in. (90 cm) print fabric, 44 in. (112 cm) wide*
* *14 in. (36 cm) elastic, ¼ in. (5 mm) wide*
* *Six ⅝-in. (15-mm) buttons*
* *Lightweight fusible interfacing*
* *Matching thread*

FOR THE SKIRT

* *Pattern K—front/back (K1)*
* *14 in. (34 cm) main fabric, 44 in. (112 cm) wide*
* *Scraps of cotton poplin/sheeting in assorted colors for the appliqués*
* *19 in. (48 cm) elastic, ½ in. (13 mm) wide*
* *Matching thread*

SIZE: 1 AND 2 YEARS

Take ⅜-in. (1-cm) seam allowances throughout, unless otherwise stated.

TO MAKE THE BLOUSE

1 Trace the pattern pieces you need from the pull-out sections onto tracing paper and cut out. Cut two front sections (left and right), one back section, two collars, two sleeves, and two 4 x 39-in. (10 x 100-cm) strips in the print fabric. Round off the collar tips using the curved edge of an eggcup. Transfer all pattern markings onto the fabric before removing the paper pattern pieces.

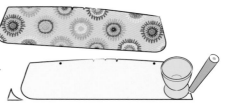

2 Stay stitch the necklines (see page 112).

3 To make the front facings, lay both front sections wrong side up on your work surface. Turn the center front edges to the wrong side by 1¼ in. (3 cm), press, and secure with basting (tacking) stitches. Turn the center front edges to the right side by 1¼ in. (3 cm) and secure with pins. Taking one front section, make a 90° angle at the neck edge by stitching from the folded edge to the dot and up to the upper edge. Trim away the seam allowance and carefully clip into the stitched corner. Turn the front facing right side out and press. Repeat for the other front section.

4 Make six buttonholes in the facing of the right front section, spacing them evenly from top neck to bottom edge.

5 With right sides together, machine stitch the front sections to the back section at the shoulder seams. Press open the seams.

6 Make and attach the collar (see page 115).

7 To make the waist ties, fold a 4 x 39-in. (10 x 100-cm) strip of fabric in half widthwise, right sides together, and machine stitch the layers together from end to end along both long edges.

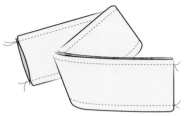

8 Trim the seam allowances, clip the corners, and turn right side out. Press and topstitch along the outer edges. Repeat for the other waist tie. Place one waist tie at each side of the front panel of the blouse at waistline notch and secure with machine stitches.

9 With right sides together, machine stitch the front sections to the back section at the side seams. Press open the seams.

10 Using the longest stitch length, machine stitch ³⁄₈ in. (1 cm) inside and along the top edges of the sleeves between the balance marks, in readiness for easing them into the armholes.

11 With right sides together, stitch the underarm seam of a sleeve. Press open and double hem the cuff (see page 113), leaving a gap in the stitching to insert elastic. Using a safety pin, feed a 7-in. (18-cm) length of elastic through the channel. Machine stitch together the ends of the elastic, push it completely into the channel, and machine stitch the opening closed. Repeat for the other sleeve.

12 Attach the sleeves (see page 114).

13 Double hem the blouse (see page 113), stitching as close as possible to the folded edge and turning the bottom edge over to the wrong side by ¹⁄₄ in. (5 mm), then again by ³⁄₈ in. (1 cm). Attach buttons to the front to finish.

TO MAKE THE SKIRT

1 Trace the pattern pieces you need from the pull-out sections onto tissue paper and cut out. Cut two front/back sections in plain fabric.

2 To make the large flower appliqué, cut a 4¾-in. (12-cm) square, a 3-in. (8-cm) square, and a circle 2⅛-in. (5.5 cm) in diameter in the scraps of assorted cotton.

3 Fold the large square in half and press, then in half again and press, and diagonally in half again and press to form a triangle.

4 Snip off the outer corner at the longest side of the triangle to form a kite shape. Roughly cut into the angle to create two half-petal outlines. Open out the flower and tightly scrunch it up into a ball to give it a delicate, crumpled look. Re-open and put to one side. Repeat steps 3 and 4 with the smaller square to create the inner petals and scrunch up the circle, too, to give it a delicate, crumpled look.

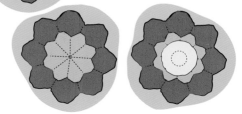

5 Machine stitch the flower to the skirt in stages, starting with the large flower head, then the inner flower, and lastly the flower center. Create stamens with French knots (see page 119).

6 To make the four small flower appliqués, cut out a 3-in. (8-cm) square, a 1¾-in. (4.5-cm) square, and a 1¼-in. (3-cm) circle in the scraps of assorted cotton for each flower, and repeat steps 3–5.

7 With right sides facing and aligning the cut edges, pin, baste (tack), and machine stitch the side seams of the skirt. Press open the seams.

8 Make a casing for the elasticated waistband (see page 116). Thread the elastic through the casing, adjusting it to fit the waist comfortably. Sew the ends together and stitch the opening closed.

9 Double hem the skirt (see page 113), turning the bottom edge over to the wrong side by ¼ in. (5 mm) and then again by ⅜ in. (1 cm).

FOR THE JACKET

* *Pattern J—front (J1), back (J2), sleeve (J3), and hood (J4)*
* *Pocket template 2 on page 125*
* *Elbow patch template on page 123*
* *Mask appliqué motifs on page 123*
* *Monogram appliqué motif on page 123*
* *32 in. (82 cm) corduroy fabric, 44 in. (112 cm) wide*
* *32 in. (82 cm) plaid cotton fabric, 44 in. (112 cm) wide, for lining*
* *Scraps of plain cotton fabric in various colors for appliqués*
* *Fusible bonding web*
* *12-in. (30-cm) open-ended zipper*
* *Matching and contrasting thread*

FOR THE SHORTS

* *Pattern I—pants front (I1), yoke front (I2), pants back (I3), and yoke back (I4)*
* *Pocket template 2 on page 125*
* *24 in. (60 cm) plain fabric, 44 in. (112 cm) wide*
* *Scraps of plaid cotton fabric for waist tie and yoke detailing*
* *19 in. (48 cm) elastic, 3/4 in. (20 mm) wide*
* *Matching and contrasting thread*

SIZE: 1 AND 2 YEARS

Take 3/8-in. (1-cm) seam allowances throughout, unless otherwise stated.

Lucha Libre

This hooded jacket with its jolly plaid lining has an eye-catching appliqué inspired by Mexican wrestlers—a "mask" motif, resembling one of the many mythical superheroes that these larger-than-life sportsmen adopt.

TO MAKE THE JACKET

1 Trace the pattern pieces you need from the pull-out sheets onto tissue paper and cut out. Cut two fronts, one back (on the folded fabric), two sleeves, two hood sections, and two 7-in. (18-cm) squares for pockets in the corduroy fabric. For the jacket lining, re-use the pattern pieces and cut two fronts, one back (on the folded fabric), two hood sections, and two sleeves in the plaid cotton fabric. Transfer all pattern markings onto the fabric before removing the paper pattern pieces.

2 To make the elbow patches, "mask" appliqué, and monogram, back the scraps of assorted plain cotton fabrics with fusible bonding web and cut out (see page 112).

3 Place one elbow patch toward the back of one sleeve on the right side of the fabric, 3½ in. (9 cm) up from the lower cut edge and 2 in. (5 cm) in from the underarm seam. Apply, following the instructions on page 118.

4 Apply the monogrammed initials to the jacket front in same way.

5 For the Mexican wrestling mask appliqué, begin with the green "oval" base, placing it at the center back of the jacket, 5 in. (13 cm) up from the lower cut edge. Next, attach the yellow horns, the red face markings, and the skull patch. Complete the appliqué by applying the facial features.

6 Cut a 1½ x 3½-in. (4 x 9-cm) strip from the plaid cotton fabric remnants to make a loop for the back neck. With wrong sides  together, fold the strip in half widthwise and press. Open out, fold both raw edges in to the center crease line, press, fold the strip in half along the center crease again, and machine stitch as close as possible along both long edges. Fold under the ends of the strip and machine stitch the loop to the back neck.

7 Make two patch pockets (see page 117). Pin and baste (tack) the pockets to the jacket fronts 2 in. (5 cm) up from the lower cut edge, inserting a tab of fabric into the side of one pocket before stitching. Topstitch close to the sides and lower edge.

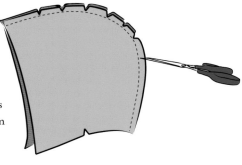

8 Lay the hood sections right sides together and machine stitch the seam. Cut out wedges along the curved seam allowance and press the seam open.

9 With right sides together, machine stitch the front sections of the jacket to the back section at the shoulder seams.

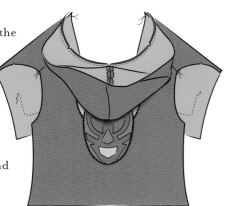

10 With right sides together, machine stitch the hood to the neck edge of the jacket, matching the notches and center seam of the hood with the shoulder seams and center back of the jacket. Cut out wedges along the curved seam allowance and press the seam open.

II Attach the sleeves (see page 114), cut out wedges along the curved seam allowance, and press the seams open.

I2 With right sides together and aligning the raw edges, lay the jacket front on the jacket back and fold the sleeves in half widthwise. Machine stitch the sleeve and side seams, and press the seams open.

I3 Repeat steps 8–12 to make the jacket lining.

I4 With right sides together, pin the outer jacket to the jacket lining, matching the seams and raw edges. Machine stitch together the hood edges and the lower edges of the jacket.

I5 Turn the jacket right side out, fold 5/8 in. (1.5 cm) of the front edges of the outer jacket and the lining separately to the inside, and carefully press.

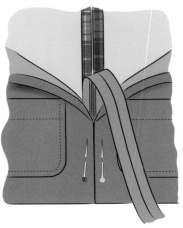

I6 Insert the zipper between the layers of the jacket's inner and outer front edges, carefully pinning and basting (tacking) it to the layers so that the teeth are covered. Machine stitch the zipper in place.

I7 Fold separately and toward one another the lower edges of the sleeves of the outer jacket and the jacket lining. Machine stitch together along the folded edge.

TO MAKE THE SHORTS

1 Trace the pattern pieces you need from the pull-out sheets onto tissue paper and cut out. When tracing the front and back pants leg patterns, draw and cut along the lines that read "cut here for shorts."

2 Pin the pattern pieces to the fabric. Cut two shorts fronts, two shorts backs, two yoke fronts (left and right), and two yoke backs (left and right) in the main fabric. Also cut two 7-in. (18-cm) squares in the main fabric for the pockets. Transfer all pattern markings onto the fabric before removing the paper pattern pieces.

3 Cut four 1½ x 7-in. (3 x 18-cm) strips from the plaid cotton fabric to make piping for the yokes. With wrong sides together, fold each strip in half widthwise and press. With cut edges aligned, lay one strip along the top edge of one shorts leg. Pin and stitch in place, stitching ¼ in. (5 mm) in from the edge. Repeat for the other leg sections.

4 With right sides together and aligning the raw edges, pin, baste (tack), and machine stitch the front and back yokes to the front and back leg sections. Press the seam allowances toward the yokes. Using a contrasting thread, topstitch the seam, stitching close to the edge.

5 With right sides together, lay the shorts fronts on the shorts backs and machine stitch the side seams together. Press the seam allowances toward the shorts backs. Using a contrasting thread, topstitch the seam close to the edge.

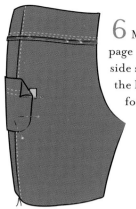

6 Make and attach the patch pockets (see page 117), placing them directly over the side seams and 4¾ in. (12 cm) up from the lower cut edge. Use contrasting thread for the topstitching.

7 With right sides together, fold the front shorts sections onto the back shorts sections and machine stitch the inner leg seams together. Press the seams open. Turn one leg right side out and pull it into the other leg, so that the right sides are facing. With raw edges aligned, pin, baste (tack), and machine stitch along the entire curved center seam from the front top edge to the back top edge. Trim the seam allowance and snip the curves.

8 Make a casing for the elastic waistband (see page 116). Thread the elastic through the casing, adjusting it to fit the waist comfortably. Sew the ends of the elastic together and stitch the gap closed.

9 Cut a 1½ x 22-in. (4 x 56-cm) strip from the plaid remnants and make a fake drawstring (see page 113). Sink stitch the middle of the drawstring onto the top center front waist and tie in a neat bow.

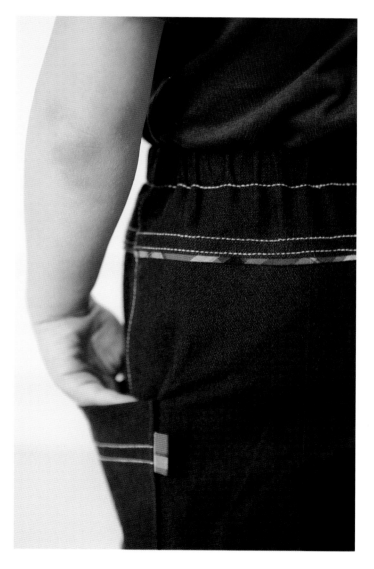

10 Double hem the shorts (see page 113), turning the bottom edge over to the wrong side by ¼ in. (5 mm) and then again by ⅜ in. (1 cm).

Art Attack

Op-Art in motion! This chic bolero and flattering dirndl skirt in a bold, kinetic paint-splash print create a truly hypnotic silhouette. The inverted pleats of the skirt are a little time consuming to make, but worth the effort. If you are short of time, reduce the fullness by simply gathering.

You will need

FOR THE BOLERO

* *Pattern O—front (O1), back (O2), and sleeve (O3)*
* *21 in. (53 cm) printed fabric, 44 in. (112 cm) wide*
* *12 in. (30 cm) lining fabric, 44 in. (112 cm) wide*
* *83½ in. (212 cm) eyelet trim (broderie anglaise), 2 in. (5 cm) wide*
* *Matching thread*

FOR THE SKIRT

* *Pattern P—front (P1), back (P2), and waistband (P3)*
* *37½ in. (95 cm) printed fabric, 44 in. (112 cm) wide*
* *One ¾-in. (18-mm) button*
* *Matching thread*

SIZE: 3, 4, AND 5 YEARS

Take ⅜-in. (1-cm) seam allowances throughout, unless otherwise stated.

TO MAKE THE BOLERO

1 Trace the pattern pieces you need from the pull-out sheets onto tissue paper and cut out. Cut two fronts, one back (on the folded fabric), and two sleeves in the print fabric. Re-using the pattern, cut one back (on the folded fabric) and two fronts in the lining fabric. Transfer all pattern markings onto the fabric before removing the paper pattern pieces.

2 With right sides together, machine stitch the front sections of the bolero to the back section at the shoulder seams.

3 With right sides facing, pin a sleeve to an armhole edge, matching the sleeve head and underarm balance marks with the shoulder seam and lower armhole balance mark of the bolero front and back. Machine stitch together, cut out wedges along the curved seam allowance, and press the seam toward the bodice.

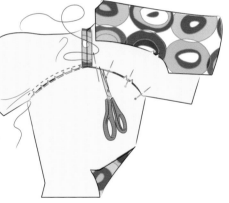

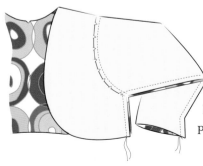

4 With right sides facing and raw edges aligned, lay the bolero front on the bolero back and fold the sleeves in half widthwise. Machine stitch the sleeve and side seams, and press the seam toward the back.

5 Double hem each sleeve (see page 113), turning the cut edge over to the wrong side by ¼ in. (5 mm) and then over again by ⅜ in. (1 cm).

6 With right sides facing, pin and machine stitch together the short edges of the eyelet trim (broderie anglaise) to form a loop and press the seam open.

7 Gather the loop to the same length as the distance all the way around the outside edge of the bolero (see page 114). With right sides together, pin the loop to the jacket edge, making sure that the gathers are evenly spaced all the way around. Baste (tack) and machine stitch in place. Press the gathered edge of the trim as flat as possible.

8 With right sides together, machine stitch the front sections of the bolero lining to the back section at the shoulder seams. Press the seams open.

9 As a folding guide, machine stitch ⅜ in. (1 cm) in from the cut edge of the bodice lining armholes. Carefully snip into the seam allowance and, using the stitching line as a guide, fold under the seam allowances and press.

10 With right sides together, machine stitch the front sections of the bolero lining to the back section at the side seams and press the seams open.

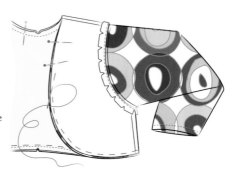

11 With right sides together, pin the lining to the bolero, matching the shoulder and side seams. Machine stitch all the way around the outside edges of the bolero. Carefully trim the seam allowances and clip the curved edges.

12 Turn the bolero right side out, carefully pulling it through one of the armholes.

13 Line up the folded armhole edges of the bodice lining with the joining seam of the jacket bodice and sleeves. Pin in place and slipstitch the openings closed, passing the needle under the stitches so that they meet edge to edge for a neat, flat finish.

14 Carefully press the outer joining seam of the bolero and lining to achieve a crisp edge.

1 Trace the pattern pieces you need from the pull-out
sections onto tissue paper and cut out. Cut one front and one
back, placing the straight (center back/center front) edges of
the pattern pieces on the folded edge of the fabric. Cut one
waistband. Transfer all pattern markings onto the fabric
before removing the paper pattern pieces.

2 With the skirt panels right
side up on your work surface,
trim 3/4 in. (2 cm) off the
extensions at the left-hand
side of the front skirt panel
and the right-hand side of
the back skirt panel so
that the "new" raw edges
are completely straight.

3 With right sides facing,
machine stitch the front and
back skirt panels together at
the right-hand side seam and
press the seam open.

4 To make the pleats on
the front and back panels of
the skirt, crease the fabric
from the outer balance marks
at the waistline to the outer
dots made with tailor's tacks
or chalk.

5 Bring the creases to the central balance mark and dot. Pin the pleats and secure by working a few machine stitches across the upper edges of the skirt to the dot.

6 Edge stitch the pleats to the dots through all thicknesses and press.

7 For the pleats at the right-hand side seam, bring the creases edge to edge over the side seam. Pin the pleats, secure by working a few machine stitches across the upper edge of the skirt, and edge stitch through all thicknesses.

8 To make the left-hand side opening of the skirt, lay the skirt panels right sides together, aligning the raw edge of the side seam and extension. Machine stitch from the hemline to dot A and from dot A to the edge of the extension.

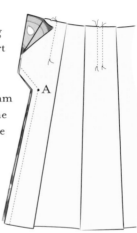

9 Fold under the front skirt panel extension, so that it lies directly underneath the topstitched pleat. Press the fold and secure with a few machine stitches across the upper edge of the skirt.

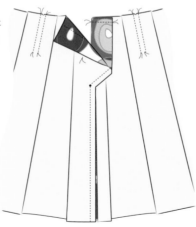

10 Fold the waistband in half widthwise, wrong sides together, and lightly press in a crease to mark the top of the waistband. Open out the waistband and machine stitch along the whole length of one long edge, 3/8 in. (1 cm) in from the raw edge. This will act as a fold-over guide when you are finishing the inside waistband.

II Aligning the raw edges and making sure that the center front and center back balance marks (on both skirt and waistband) are matched up, pin the unstitched right side of the waistband to the right side of the skirt. Also make sure that the waistband extends 3/8 in. (1 cm) out from the edge of the skirt opening extension on the left-hand side of the back skirt panel. Machine stitch together.

I2 Open out the folded waistband and fold it back on itself, so that the right sides face each other. Aligning the raw edges of the waistband ends, pin and machine stitch together. Snip the seam allowance diagonally at the corners.

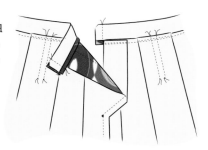

I3 Turn the waistband right side out and fold under the seam allowance of the inside waistband, using the line of machine stitches as a guide. Pin and slipstitch the opening closed.

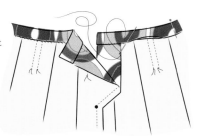

I4 Make a machine buttonhole 3/8 in. (1 cm) in from the edge, and attach a button to the end of the waistband.

I5 Double hem the skirt (see page 113), turning the lower edge to the wrong side by 1/4 in. (5 mm) and again by 3/4 in. (2 cm). Hand stitch the hem in place or machine stitch it along the folded edge.

Teatime Treat

Even in today's high-speed world, there is still room for the ever-so-traditional "little girl's" dress. Here, the humble kitchen apron—another classic from a bygone era—is elevated to "kiddie couture" status, in the form of a flower-strewn panel that floats about the waist. Fashioned from a vintage tablecloth (so much easier than embroidering the motifs yourself!), it is coordinated with a dainty floral print and eyelet trim (broderie anglaise).

You will need

* *Pattern Q—front bodice (Q1), skirt front (Q2), back bodice (Q3), back skirt (Q4), front waistband (Q5), and back tie (Q6)*

* *Pocket template 1 on page 125*

* *37½ in. (95 cm) print fabric, 44 in. (112 cm) wide*

* *11 in. (28 cm) lining fabric, 44 in. (112 cm) wide*

* *24 in. (60 cm) plain fabric, 36 in. (90 cm) wide, or embroidered tablecloth, for apron*

* *70 in. (175 cm) eyelet trim (broderie anglaise), 1½ in. (4 cm) wide, for dress*

* *18½ in. (47 cm) eyelet trim (broderie anglaise), 2⅜ in. (6 cm) wide, for apron*

* *11-in. (28-cm) zipper*

* *Matching thread*

SIZE: 3, 4, AND 5 YEARS

Take ⅜-in. (1-cm) seam allowances throughout, unless otherwise stated.

1 Trace the pattern pieces you need from the pull-out sheets onto tissue paper and cut out. Cut one bodice front and one skirt front in the print fabric, placing the straight (center front) edges of the pattern pieces on the folded edge of the fabric. Cut two skirt backs and a left and a right bodice back in print fabric. Cut one bodice front, placing the straight (center front) edge of the pattern piece on the folded edge of the fabric, and a left and right bodice back in lining fabric. Transfer all pattern markings onto the fabric before removing the paper pattern pieces.

2 For the apron panel, cut a 12 x 18½-in. (30.5 x 47-cm) rectangle from the plain fabric (if using an embroidered tablecloth for the apron panel, make sure that any embroidered motifs are centrally placed). Cut two back ties, one front waistband on the "cross" (the diagonal grain of the fabric), and a 5½-in. (14-cm) square (apron pocket) in the remaining apron fabric.

3 Stay stitch the front and back necklines of the bodice ¼ in. (5 mm) in from the cut edges to prevent them from stretching (see page 112). Repeat for the bodice lining.

4 With right sides together, fold a back tie in half widthwise. Machine stitch along its length and the diagonal edge, leaving the straight end open. Snip the corners, turn right side out, and press. Repeat for the remaining back tie.

5 Machine stitch the straight end of a back tie to the right side of each bodice back section, stitching ⅜ in. (1 cm) in from the raw edge of the waistline.

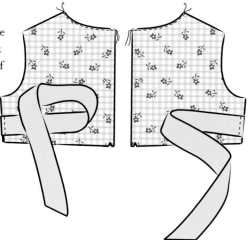

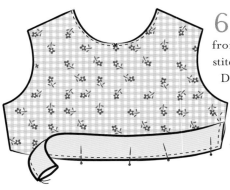

6 With wrong sides together, fold the front waistband in half widthwise. Stay stitch ¼ in. (5 mm) in from the cut edges. Do not press the fold. Pin and machine stitch the front waistband to the bodice front, aligning the long stitched edge of the front waistband with the bottom of the bodice.

7 Machine stitch the bodice front to the bodice back sections at the shoulder seams, press open the seams, and put to one side.

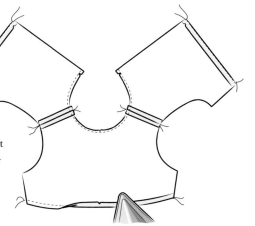

8 Machine stitch the bodice lining front to the bodice lining back sections at the shoulder seams and press open the seams. Machine stitch ⅜ in. (1 cm) in from the lower cut edge of each section of bodice lining. Carefully fold the fabric under to the wrong side along this stitching line, and press.

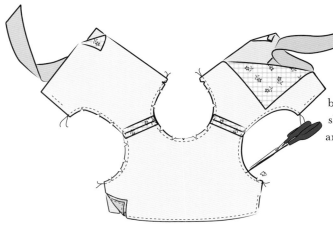

9 With right sides together, pin the lining to the bodice, matching the center fronts and backs and shoulder seams. Machine stitch all the way around the armholes and necklines. Carefully clip all curved edges.

10 Turn the bodice lining to the inside by pulling each back section through the shoulder areas. Carefully press the finished seams to achieve crisp edges.

II Open out the front bodice/bodice lining and back bodice/bodice lining on the left side. Placing the four sections right sides together and aligning the raw edges, stitch the side seam in one continuous action. Press open the side seam. Repeat for the right side. Turn the bodice lining back in place, press, and put to one side.

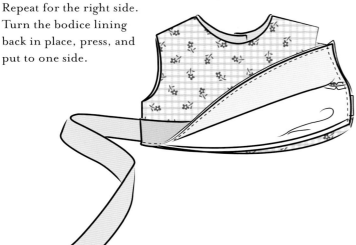

12 Double hem the lower long edge of the apron panel (see page 113), turning over ¼ in. (5 mm) and then ⅜ in. (1 cm) to the wrong side. Pin the length of 2⅜-in. (6-cm) eyelet trim (broderie anglaise) across and above the bottom of the apron panel and stitch in place. Double hem the apron panel sides, turning ¼ in. (5 mm) and then ⅜ in. (1 cm) to the wrong side. Press and put to one side.

13 Make the patch pocket for the apron (see page 117). Attach the pocket to the apron front, about 3½ in. (9 cm) down from the upper raw edge; the exact position will depend on the position of the embroidered motifs, if used.

14 Mark the center front of the apron by making a tiny snip in the seam allowance. Gather up the apron along the top raw edge to a width of 9½ in. (24 cm) (see page 114). Secure the gathering threads, press flat the gathered seam allowance, and put the apron to one side.

15 With right sides together and taking a ⅝-in. (1.5-cm) seam allowance, machine stitch the back skirt panels together at the center back seam, from the hem edge to the balance mark snip. Press open the seam, folding under ⅝ in. (1.5 cm); the unstitched edges will form part of the opening for the zipper.

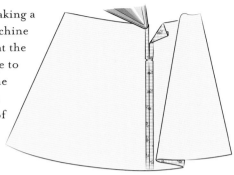

16 With right sides together, machine stitch the skirt front to the skirt back at the side seams. Press open the seams.

17 Using the longest stitch length, machine stitch ⅝ in. (1.5 cm) in from the bottom edge of the skirt. Fold the fabric to the wrong side along this stitching line, then baste (tack) and press to hold in place. To finish the hem, topstitch through all thicknesses about ⅜ in. (1 cm) in from the folded edge. Remove the basting (tacking) and guideline stitches.

18 Pin the length of 1½-in. (4-cm) eyelet trim (broderie anglaise) to the wrong side of the base of the skirt, so that it hangs down below the hem, and stitch it in place.

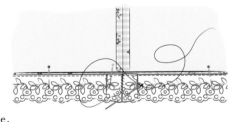

19 Open out the bodice lining. With right sides together and matching the centers, pin the gathered apron to the lower edge of the dress bodice front. Baste (tack) and machine stitch the apron in place, making sure the gathers are evenly spaced.

20 Gather the skirt to the same width as the bottom of the bodice (see page 114). With right sides together, matching the centers and side seams, pin the skirt to the lower edge of the bodice, with the apron sandwiched between the layers, making sure the gathers are evenly spaced all around. Baste (tack) in place and then machine stitch. Press the waistline seam toward the bodice.

21 Line up the folded and pre-stitched bottom edge of the lining with the waistline seam of the bodice and skirt. Pin and slipstitch in place, passing the needle under the stitches so that they meet edge to edge for a neat, flat finish.

22 Press under 5/8 in. (1.5 cm) along the center back edges. With the pressed center back edges meeting, place the zipper underneath the dress bodice and skirt and carefully baste (tack) it in place. Following the basting stitches, machine stitch the zipper to the dress through all thicknesses. Fold over the top ends of the zipper to finish.

Pretty in Pink

This light summer coat is an ideal wardrobe basic and will look good in either plain or printed fabric. Made in waterproof fabric, it is guaranteed to cheer up your little one on a rainy day. For added novelty and color interest, you could make the pockets, collar, and facings in a contrasting fabric. To soften the classic, tailored look, the coat featured here is made in a whimsical floral print.

You will need

* Pattern L—front (L1), back (L2), sleeve (L3), and collar (L4)
* Pocket template 4 on page 125
* Pocket flap template 5 on page 125
* 50 in. (125 cm) printed fabric, 44 in. (112 cm) wide
* 64½ in. (164 cm) bias binding, 1 in. (25 mm) wide
* Mediumweight fusible interfacing
* Seven ¾-in. (20-mm) buttons
* Matching thread

SIZE: 3, 4, AND 5 YEARS

Take ⅜-in. (1-cm) seam allowances throughout, unless otherwise stated.

A jacket pattern is used to make this coat, so you need to alter the pattern before you cut it out in paper. The front and back sections of the jacket need to be lengthened, the back sections need to be extended in order to create a back vent, and the "coat" fronts require facings.

1 To lengthen the front panel of the jacket, trace pattern piece L1 from the pull-out sheets provided onto tissue paper. Extend the straight center line by 6 in. (15 cm) to point A and the diagonal line at the side seam by 6 in. (15 cm) to point B. Redraw the hemline from point A to point B, matching the curved hemline of the original jacket pattern. Cut out the paper pattern along the redrawn lines.

2 To make the front facing pattern, take an additional sheet of paper and trace off the central area of the new, extended front pattern piece. Draw a line from the neck edge to the hemline, parallel to and 2¾ in. (7 cm) in from the straight central edge. Draw a line from the shoulder edge to the straight central edge, parallel to and 2 in. (5 cm) in from the curved neck edge. Place a round plate over the corner created by these lines so that the rim touches the two sides. Draw around the plate to round off the corner. Cut out the paper pattern along the redrawn lines.

3 To lengthen the back panel of the jacket, trace pattern piece L2 from the pull-out sheets provided onto tissue paper. Extend the diagonal line at the side seam by 6 in. (15 cm) to point A and the straight center line by 6 in. (15 cm) to point B. Redraw the hemline from point A to point B, matching the curved hemline of the original jacket pattern.

4 To form the back vent, measure 8 in. (20 cm) up the straight center line from point B to point C. Draw a 2³⁄₈-in. (6-cm) horizontal line at a 90° angle from point B to point E and draw a 7-in. (18-cm) vertical line (at a 90° angle) from point E up to point D. Draw a line from point D to point C to complete the back vent extension.

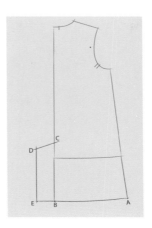

5 Add a ³⁄₈-in. (1-cm) seam allowance to the center back by drawing a line down from the top neck edge to the diagonal line C to D. Cut out the paper pattern along the redrawn lines.

6 Cut two front sections, two front facings, two back sections, two sleeves, two collars (upper and under), and four 6¹⁄₂ x 7¹⁄₂-in. (17 x 19-cm) pieces for flap patch pockets in the print fabric. Transfer all pattern markings onto the fabric before removing the paper pattern pieces.

7 Stay stitch all necklines ³/₈ in. (1 cm) in from the cut edges to prevent them from stretching (see page 112).

8 Apply interfacing to the wrong sides of the facings (see page 112). Pin a length of bias binding to the inner edge of each front facing. Edge stitch the bindings in place, fold under the narrow top ends of the facings by ³/₈ in. (1 cm), and put to one side (see page 118).

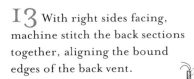

9 Pin a length of bias binding to the long edge of each back vent. Edge stitch the bindings in place (see page 118).

10 Make a patch pocket from one of the 6¹/₂ x 7¹/₂-in. (17 x 19-cm) pieces of fabric (see page 117). Machine stitch the patch pocket to the coat front approximately 2³/₄ in. (7 cm) in from the center front raw edge and 4³/₄ in. (12 cm) up from the bottom edge.

11 Make a pocket flap from one of the 6¹/₂ x 7¹/₂-in. (17 x 19-cm) pieces of fabric (see page 117). Turn it right side out, press, topstitch around the edges and make two diagonal buttonholes. Attach the pocket flap ³/₈ in. (1 cm) above the patch pocket (see page 117).

12 Repeat steps 10–11 to make the pocket for the other front section, using the two remaining 6¹/₂ x 7¹/₂-in. (17 x 19-cm) pieces of fabric.

13 With right sides facing, machine stitch the back sections together, aligning the bound edges of the back vent.

14 Open out the back sections and press the seam allowances and the vents in one direction. Turn the back of the coat right side up, press the crease again, and sink stitches diagonally through all thicknesses at the upper end of the vent.

15 With right sides together, machine stitch the coat front to the back at the shoulder seams.

16 Apply interfacing to the wrong side of the top collar and make the collar (see page 115). Attach the collar to the coat (see page 115).

17 With right sides together, pin the facings to the front and neck edges of the coat and machine stitch through all thicknesses. Trim the seam allowances, clip the corners, and snip the curved edges. Turn the facings to the inside and press. Stitch the folded-under ends of the facings to the shoulder seam allowances.

18 With right sides together, machine stitch the coat front to the back at the side seams.

19 Using the longest machine stitch, stitch around the sleeve heads between the balance marks to gather them slightly and help ease them into the armholes later (see page 114).

20 With right sides together, fold the sleeves widthwise, align the raw edges, and machine stitch the underarm seams. Finish the lower edge of the sleeve with a 1¼-in. (3-cm) single hem. Repeat for the other sleeve. Attach the sleeves to the coat body (see page 114).

21 To hem the coat, turn the front facings and the vents to the outside. Aligning the lower edges of the coat with the lower edges of the facings, pin, baste (tack), and machine stitch along the lower edge. Trim the lower edges of the facings, snip off the corners, and turn the facings inside. Press the facings, press up the hem by 1¼ in. (3 cm), and slipstitch it in place.

22 Make three buttonholes in the front of the coat, spacing them 5½ in. (13 cm) apart, and attach buttons to the front and pockets.

Spice Island

Shiver me timbers! This certainly is the perfect look for a pint-size buccaneer. The store-bought T-shirt is embellished with a whimsical take on the "Jolly Roger"—a smirking skull, with crossed cutlass blades replacing the typical crossbones—while the Indian cotton pants, in a rich and spicy geometric batik print, add a touch of exoticism. The *trompe l'oeil* fly front provides a note of authenticity and is very easy to make.

You will need

FOR THE T-SHIRT

* Store-bought T-shirt
* Appliqué motifs on page 124
* Scraps of cotton poplin/sheeting in assorted colors
* Fusible bonding web
* Matching or contrasting thread

FOR THE PANTS

* Pattern N—front (N1), back (N2), waistband (N3)
* Pocket template 4 on page 125
* 36 in. (90 cm) print fabric, 44 in. (112 cm) wide
* Mediumweight fusible interfacing
* 1½ in. (4 cm) contrast tape
* 14 in. (36 cm) elastic, ¾ in. (18 mm) wide
* Matching thread

SIZE: 3, 4, AND 5 YEARS

Take ⅜-in. (1-cm) seam allowances throughout, unless otherwise stated.

TO MAKE THE T-SHIRT

I Trace the skull, eye patch, bandana, and cutlass motifs onto thin card and cut out. Carefully cut out the eye socket and nostrils of the skull with a craft knife. Cut squares of fusible bonding web large enough to accommodate all the motifs. Lay the squares on the wrong side of your appliqué fabrics, adhesive side down, and press with a hot iron to heat bond (see page 112).

2 Turn the card templates over, place them on the paper-backed side of the appliqué fabrics, and draw around them with a pencil. Draw around the cutlass twice, flipping the template the second time. Carefully cut out the motifs and put them to one side.

3 Decide on the position of the skull, and apply it to the front of the garment (see page 118). Apply the eye patch, eye socket, nostrils, and bandana in the same way, changing the thread color if you wish. Stitch a sly grin onto the skull, using small, dense machine zigzag stitches.

4 Decide on the position of the crossed cutlass blades and attach them to the T-shirt in the same way as the other appliqué motifs.

5 Cut the blade off the card cutlass template and place the hilt on the paper-backed side of contrasting appliqué fabric. Draw around the template once, flip the template, and repeat. Carefully cut out the motifs, and apply them on top of the cutlass motifs that are already attached to the T-shirt. Using a small zigzag stitch, sew all the way around the cutlass motifs, changing the thread color if you wish.

1 Trace the pattern pieces you need from the pull-out sections onto tissue paper and cut out. Cut two front and two back pant sections, one waistband (on the folded fabric), and two 6½ x 7½-in. (17 x 19-cm) rectangles for pockets in the print fabric. Transfer all pattern markings onto the fabric before removing the paper pattern pieces.

2 Back the center front area of the waistband with mediumweight fusible interfacing (see page 112).

3 To make a patch pocket, fold under ¾ in. (2 cm) to the wrong side along one short edge of the fabric rectangle and topstitch through all thicknesses. Complete the patch pocket (see page 117).

4 Lay the pocket on top of a back leg, 2 in. (5 cm) down from the raw edge of the waistline. Insert a folded 1½-in. (4-cm) strip of contrast tape into the side for the pocket tab and topstitch close to the edges of the pocket. Repeat steps 3–4 to make the pocket for the other leg.

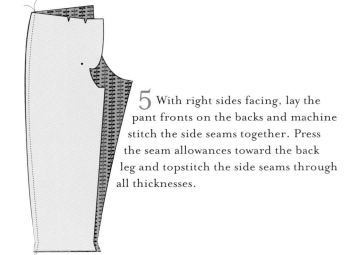

5 With right sides facing, lay the pant fronts on the backs and machine stitch the side seams together. Press the seam allowances toward the back leg and topstitch the side seams through all thicknesses.

6 With right sides together, fold one front section of the pants onto the back section and machine stitch the inner leg seam. Press the seam open. Repeat for the other leg.

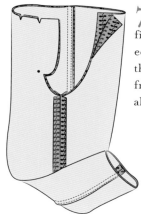

7 Turn one leg right side out and pull it into the other finished leg, so that the right sides are facing. With raw edges aligned, pin, baste (tack), and machine stitch along the curved center seam, from the back top edge to the fly front dot marked on the pattern piece. Trim the seam allowance on the curve.

8 Make a fake fly front (see page 116).

9 Attach the waistband, leaving a gap to thread through the elastic. Insert the elastic and hand stitch the opening in the waistband closed (see page 116).

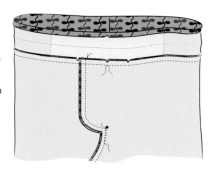

10 On each pant leg, press hem 3/4 in. (2 cm) to the wrong side and machine stitch in place.

Little Miss Marguerite

This delightful two-piece ensemble pays homage to the humble daisy. The store-bought T-shirt is embellished with a cloud of "blossom" that floats gracefully across the body on a light summer breeze, while cookie-cutter flower heads trim a billowing dirndl skirt that can be instantly transformed into a playful, multi-pocketed mini.

You will need

FOR THE T-SHIRT

* Store-bought T-shirt
* Tree motif on page 120
* 8-in. (20-cm) square of cotton poplin/sheeting
* 20-in. (50-cm) length of guipure "daisy" trim
* Fabric glue
* Matching thread

FOR THE SKIRT

* Pattern R—front/back skirt (R1)
* Daisy motif on page 120
* 24 in. (60 cm) striped fabric, 36 in. (90 cm) wide
* 20 in. (50 cm) spotted fabric, 36 in. (90 cm) wide
* 16-in. (40-cm) square of cotton poplin/sheeting for appliqués
* Fusible bonding web
* 23 in. (58 cm) elastic, 3/4 in. (18 mm) wide
* Eight 3/4-in. (20-mm) buttons
* Matching thread

SIZE: 3, 4, AND 5 YEARS

Take 3/8-in. (1-cm) seam allowances throughout, unless otherwise stated.

TO MAKE THE T-SHIRT

1 Trace the tree motif on page 120 onto thin card and cut out. Cut a square of fusible bonding web large enough to accommodate the motif. Lay the square on the wrong side of your appliqué fabric, adhesive side down, and press with a hot iron to heat bond (see page 112).

2 Place the card template on the paper-backed side of the appliqué fabric and draw around it with a pencil. Carefully cut out the motif with a craft knife.

3 Decide on the position of the motif, apply it (see page 118), and zizzag stitch all the way around. When stitching on the front and the right side of the motif, it is advisable to turn the T-shirt inside out to avoid accidentally stitching into the back panel of the garment.

4 Carefully separate the flowers of the guipure "daisy" trim and attach them, one by one, to the garment with fabric glue or small hand stitches.

TO MAKE THE SKIRT

1 Trace the pattern piece from the pull-out sheets onto tissue paper and cut out. Carefully transfer the daisy outlines before cutting out the pattern, as their exact positions are essential in order to place the appliqués accurately on the skirt and skirt lining.

2 Cut two front/back sections for the skirt and two 3½ x 16-in. (9 x 40-cm) strips for the waistband in the striped fabric, and two front/back sections in the spotted fabric for the skirt lining. Notch the top edges of all fabric pieces to indicate the center front and center back.

3 Back the square of appliqué fabric with fusible bonding web (see page 112), draw around the daisy template 16 times, and carefully cut out the daisies.

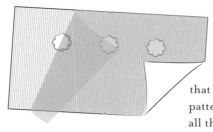

4 Lay one skirt section right side up on your work surface and place three daisies below the waistline, laying the paper pattern on top of the fabric to check that each daisy is in the correct position. Remove the paper pattern, fix the appliqués in place with a hot iron, and sew all the way around the motifs using a small zigzag stitch. Repeat for the other skirt section.

5 With right sides facing, machine stitch the front and back panels of the skirt together at the side seams. Press open the seams. Apply a daisy over each side seam, level with the daisies in the previous step (see page 118).

6 Lay a skirt lining section right side up on your work surface and apply three daisies over the hemline (see page 118). Repeat for the other lining section.

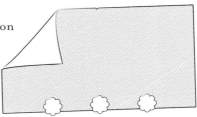

7 With right sides facing, machine stitch the front and back panels of the skirt lining together at the side seams. Press open the seams. Apply a daisy over each side seam and hemline, level with the daisies in the previous step.

8 With right sides together, machine stitch the skirt to the lining at the hem, matching the side seams and aligning the raw edges. Open out the skirt and the lining and press the seam flat. Turn the lining back in place, press the hem edge, and topstitch.

9 Matching the side seams, machine stitch the skirt to the lining 5/8 in. (1.5 cm) down from the raw waist edges to secure the layers.

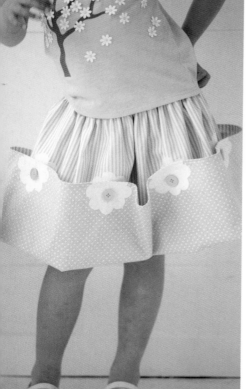

10 Turn the skirt inside out and lay it flat on your work surface. Matching the outlines, place the card template over an appliquéd daisy on the hemline, and mark the center point with a pencil. Make a buttonhole, using this mark as the starting point. Repeat for the remaining daisies.

II Turn the skirt right side out and lay it flat on your work surface. Matching the outlines, place the card template over an appliquéd daisy below the waistline, mark the center point with a pencil, and attach a button. Repeat for the remaining daisies.

I2 With right sides together, machine stitch the short ends of the waistband together to form a loop. Press open the seams. With wrong sides together, fold the loop in half widthwise and press in a crease; this will be the top edge of the waistband. Open out, fold under 3/8 in. (I cm) to the wrong side along the bottom edge, and press.

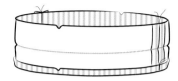

I3 Gather the skirt to the same circumference as the waistband (see page II4).

I4 With right sides facing, attach the unfolded edge of the waistband to the upper edge of the skirt, matching the side seams, center front, and center back notches, and making sure that the gathers are evenly spaced all the way around. Baste (tack) in place and then machine stitch.

I5 Press the gathered seam allowances flat, turn the waistband to the inside, and edge stitch the waistband in place, leaving a gap in the stitching to insert the elastic.

I6 Thread the elastic through the casing, adjusting it to fit the waist comfortably. Sew the ends together and stitch the opening closed.

Modern Romance

Inspired by the little princesses of folklore and fairytale, this contemporary A-line dress is enhanced with delicate ribbon detailing that can be criss-crossed at the front or back of the bodice. The neckline and armholes are finished with neat, color-matched bindings that eliminate the need for fussy facings and create a charming summer frock that is as light as a feather.

You will need

* Pattern M—front (M1) and back (M2)
* 25½ in. (65 cm) floral print fabric, 54 in. (138 cm) wide
* 53 in. (135 cm) bias binding, 1 in. (25 mm) wide
* 118 in. (300 cm) grosgrain (petersham) ribbon, ¼ in. (5 mm) wide
* Five ¾-in. (18-mm) buttons
* Matching thread

SIZE: **3**, 4, AND 5 YEARS

Take ⅜-in. (1-cm) seam allowances throughout, unless otherwise stated.

I Trace the pattern pieces you need from the pull-out sheets onto tissue paper and cut out. Cut one front (on the folded fabric) and two back sections in the floral print fabric. Transfer all pattern markings onto the fabric before removing the paper pattern pieces.

2 Stay stitch the necklines and armholes ¼ in. (5 mm) in from the cut edges to prevent them from stretching while you are making the dress.

3 To make the back facings, turn the center back edges to the wrong side by 1 in. (2.5 cm) and press. Turn the back edges to the wrong side again by 1 in. (2.5 cm), press, secure the double folds with basting (tacking) stitches, and machine stitch across the folds ¼ in. (5 mm) down from the neck edges.

4 With right sides together, machine stitch the front dress section to the back dress sections at the shoulder seams. Press open the seams.

5 Apply a 17¾-in. (45-cm) length of bias binding around the neckline (see page 118), carefully folding under the ends of the binding for a neat finish.

6 Cut six 1½-in. (4-cm) lengths of grosgrain (petersham) ribbon to make loops for the dress front. Fold each length in half. Machine stitch three loops to one side of the dress front—one at waist level, one ⅝ in. (1.5 cm) below the armhole, and one in between. Repeat for the other side.

7 With right sides together, machine stitch the front dress section to the back dress sections at the side seams. Press open the seams and finish each armhole with a 17¾-in. (45-cm) length of bias binding (see page 118).

8 To hem the dress, remove the basting (tacking) stitches from one back facing and open out the folds. Turn the facing to the outside at the lower edge and machine stitch across the facing at the hem point.

9 Trim away the facing close to the stitching. Repeat steps 8 and 9 for the other back facing.

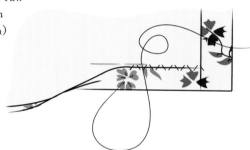

10 Turn both back facings to the inside and press. Press up the hem by 1 in. (2.5 cm). Press under the raw edge of the hem by ¼ in. (5 mm) and stitch the hem in place.

11 Make six vertical buttonholes in the facing of the left back section, spacing them evenly from top to bottom. Attach buttons to the right back facing.

12 To finish, thread the remaining grosgrain (petersham) ribbon through the loops in a criss-cross fashion and tie in a neat bow.

Spring Showers

This delectable, vintage-style dress is guaranteed to appeal to all ages. The bodice is fully lined, removing the need to make fiddly bindings or facings for the neck and armholes. And with a simple trim for the hem, dainty motifs cut from guipure lace remnants for the flower-strewn bodice, and grosgrain (petersham) ribbon for the waist ties, this kiddies classic is instantly elevated to special occasion status.

You will need

* Pattern Q—front bodice (Q1), front skirt (Q2), back bodice (Q3), and back skirt (Q4)

* 36 in. (90 cm) print fabric, 50 in. (128 cm) wide

* 20 in. (50 cm) plain fabric, 36 in. (90 cm) wide

* Scraps of guipure lace for bodice appliqué

* 70 in. (178 cm) eyelet trim (broderie anglaise), 1½ in. (4 cm) wide

* 55 in. (140 cm) grosgrain (petersham) ribbon, 1 in. (25 mm) wide

* 11-in. (28-cm) zipper

* Matching thread

SIZE: 3, 4, AND **5** YEARS

Take ⅜-in. (1-cm) seam allowances throughout, unless otherwise stated.

I Trace the pattern pieces you need from the pull-out sheets onto tissue paper and cut out. Cut two front bodices (on the folded fabric) and four back bodice sections in plain fabric. Cut one front skirt (on the folded fabric) and two back skirt sections in print fabric. Transfer all pattern markings onto the fabric and snip into the fabric to mark all center front and center back positions before removing the paper pattern pieces.

2 Stay stitch the front and back necklines of the bodice and bodice lining ¼ in. (5 mm) in from the cut edges to prevent them from stretching during make (see page 112).

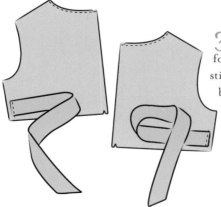

3 Cut the grosgrain (petersham) ribbon for the back waist ties in half. Machine stitch one length to the side of a bodice back section, placing it ⅜ in. (1 cm) in from the raw edge of the waistline and ⅜ in. (1 cm) up from the bottom raw edge. Repeat for the other bodice back.

4 Machine stitch the bodice front to the bodice back at the shoulder seams, press the seams open, and put to one side.

5 Machine stitch the front and back sections of the bodice lining together at the shoulder seams and press the seams open. As a folding guide, machine stitch ³/₈ in. (1 cm) up from the bottom cut edges of the bodice lining. Following the stitch line, carefully fold under the seam allowances and press.

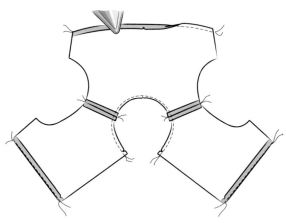

6 With right sides together, pin the lining to the bodice, matching the front and back centers and shoulder seams. Machine stitch all the way around the armholes and necklines. Carefully clip all the curved edges.

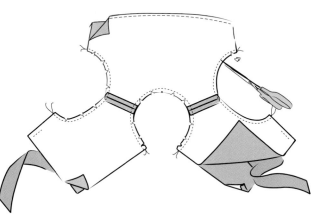

7 Turn the bodice lining to the inside by pulling each back section through the shoulder areas. Carefully press the finished seams to achieve crisp edges.

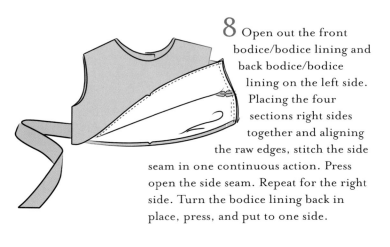

8 Open out the front bodice/bodice lining and back bodice/bodice lining on the left side. Placing the four sections right sides together and aligning the raw edges, stitch the side seam in one continuous action. Press open the side seam. Repeat for the right side. Turn the bodice lining back in place, press, and put to one side.

9 With right sides together and taking a 5/8-in. (1.5-cm) seam allowance, machine stitch the back skirt panels together at the center back seam, from the hem edge to the balance mark snip. Press open the seam and fold under the unstitched sections by 5/8 in. (1.5 cm); these edges will form part of the opening for the zipper.

10 With right sides together, machine stitch the skirt front to the back at the side seams. Press open the seams.

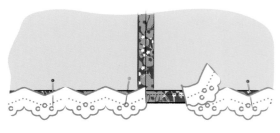

11 Using the longest stitch length, machine stitch 5/8 in. (1.5 cm) in from the bottom edge of the skirt. Fold the fabric to the wrong side along this stitching line, then baste (tack) and press to hold in place. To finish the hem, topstitch through all thicknesses about 3/8 in. (1 cm) in from the folded edge. Remove the basting and guideline stitches.

12 Pin the length of eyelet trim (broderie anglaise) to the wrong side of the base of the skirt, so that it hangs down below the hem, and machine stitch it in place.

13 Following the instructions on page 114, gather the skirt to the same width as the bottom of the bodice. With right sides together, matching the centers and side seams, pin the skirt to the lower edge of the bodice, making sure that the gathers are evenly spaced all around. Baste (tack) in place and then machine stitch. Press the waistline seam toward the bodice.

14 Line up the folded and pre-stitched bottom edge of the lining with the waistline seam of the bodice and skirt. Pin in place and slipstitch the opening closed, passing the needle under the stitches so that they meet edge to edge for a neat, flat finish.

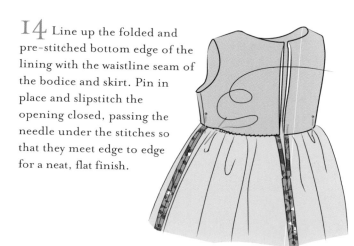

15 Press under the center back edges to the wrong side by ⅝ in. (1.5 cm). With the pressed center back edges meeting, place the zipper underneath the dress bodice and skirt, and carefully baste (tack) it in place. Following the basting stitches, machine stitch the zipper to the dress through all thicknesses. Fold over the top ends of the zipper to finish.

You will need

FOR THE VEST (WAISTCOAT)

* *Pattern S—front (S1), back (S2)*
* *Pocket template 1 on page 125*
* *20-in. (50-cm) square of print fabric*
* *18 in. (45 cm) plain fabric, 57 in. (145 cm) wide*
* *4³⁄₄ in. (12 cm) bias binding, ⁵⁄₈ in. (15 mm) wide*
* *1¹⁄₂ in. (4 cm) grosgrain (petersham) ribbon, ⁵⁄₈ in. (15 mm) wide*
* *Lightweight fusible interfacing*
* *Three ³⁄₄-in. (20-mm) buttons, one in a contrasting color*

FOR THE PANTS

* *Pattern N—front (N1), back (N2), waistband (N3)*
* *Pocket template 4 on page 125*
* *Pocket flap template 5 on page 125*
* *32 in. (80 cm) cotton twill fabric, 62 in. (156 cm) wide*
* *Mediumweight fusible interfacing*
* *Nine ³⁄₄-in. (20-mm) buttons, three in contrasting colors*
* *3 in. (8 cm) herringbone tape, 1 in. (25 mm) wide*
* *4 in. (10 cm) bias binding, ⁵⁄₈ in. (15 mm) wide*
* *15 in. (38 cm) elastic, ³⁄₄ in. (18 mm) wide*
* *Matching and contrasting threads*

SIZE: 3, 4, AND 5 YEARS

Take ³⁄₈-in. (1-cm) seam allowances throughout, unless otherwise stated.

Road to Morocco

This fresh, dazzling white outfit will come as a welcome relief as the temperature soars in high summer. Freshly laundered cotton twill pants feature multiple pockets with button details playfully picked out in primary bright colors. The fully lined vest (waistcoat), with adjustable ties at the back, has a splendid tile-patterned front, a dainty coin pocket for holding holiday pocket money or essential sun shades, and a cheeky contrast buttonhole.

TO MAKE THE VEST (WAISTCOAT)

I Trace the pattern pieces you need from the pull-out sections onto tissue paper and cut out. Cut two fronts in print fabric, and two fronts and two backs in plain fabric. Transfer all pattern markings onto the fabric before removing the paper pattern pieces. Cut two 3 x 12-in. (8 x 30-cm) strips from the plain fabric remnants for the back ties.

2 Back the center front area of the vest (waistcoat) lining panel that will hold the buttonholes with lightweight fusible interfacing (see page 112).

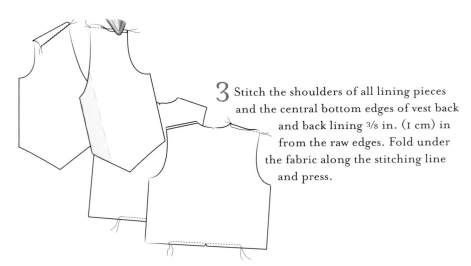

3 Stitch the shoulders of all lining pieces and the central bottom edges of vest back and back lining ³⁄₈ in. (1 cm) in from the raw edges. Fold under the fabric along the stitching line and press.

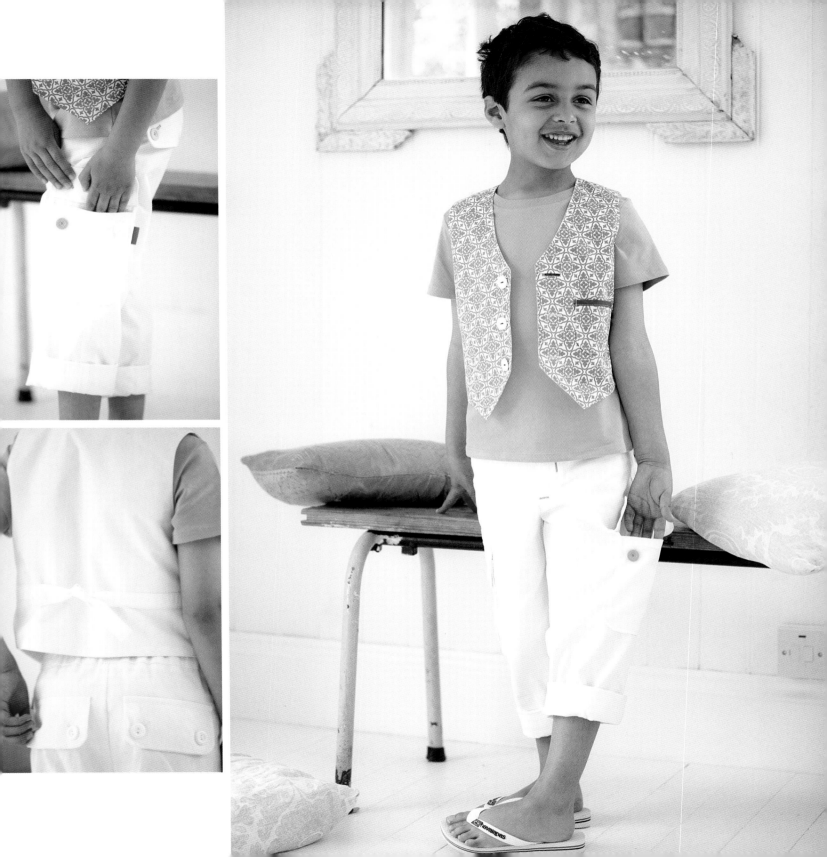

4 To make the patch pocket, attach bias binding to one edge of the square (see page 118). Complete the patch pocket, following the instructions on page 117, and attach to the front panel of the vest 3½ in. (9 cm) in from the pointed hem and 2⅜ in. (6 cm) in from the side.

5 Make back ties from the two 3 x 12-in. (8 x 30-cm) strips (see page 113).

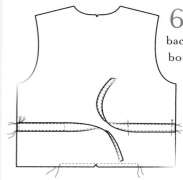

6 Pin a tie to the side of the vest back, 3 in. (8 cm) up from the bottom raw edge. Following the original topstitching on the tie, restitch through all thicknesses for 4⅜ in. (11 cm), then across the width of the tie, and back toward the side of the vest back. Repeat for the other side.

7 With right sides facing, lay the vest fronts on the back, machine stitch the side seams together, and press the seams open. Repeat for the vest lining.

8 With vest and lining right sides facing, stitch together all edges except for the shoulder edges. Leave an opening in the back hem for turning the vest right side out.

9 Trim the seam allowances, clip the corners and curved edges, turn the vest right side out through the opening, and slipstitch the opening closed, passing the needle through the pre-stitched rows for a neat, even finish. Press all edges of the vest for a crisp finish.

10 Place the vest fronts on the vest back, right sides facing. Machine stitch together along the shoulder seams. Trim off the corners of the seam allowances diagonally.

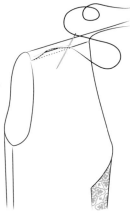

11 Slide the seam allowances under the folded shoulder edges of the lining and slipstitch the openings closed, passing the needle through the pre-stitched rows for a neat, even finish.

12 Make three buttonholes in the left vest front (one in contrasting thread), spacing them evenly, and attach buttons to the right vest front to finish.

1 Trace the pattern pieces you need from the pull-out sections onto tissue paper and cut out. Cut two front and two back pant sections, one waistband (on the folded fabric), and six 6½ x 7½-in. (17 x 19-cm) rectangles for the pockets in the cotton twill fabric. Transfer all pattern markings onto the fabric before removing the paper pattern pieces. Back the center front area of the waistband with mediumweight fusible interfacing (see page 112).

2 To make a pocket bag, fold under ¾ in. (2 cm) to the wrong side along one short edge of a fabric rectangle and topstitch. Complete the pocket following the instructions on page 117. Repeat for the other pocket bag and put to one side.

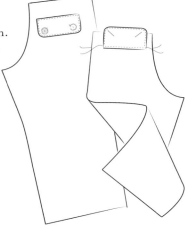

3 Make four pocket flaps from the remaining rectangles (see page 117). Turn right side out, press, topstitch around the edges, and make two diagonal buttonholes.

4 Attach one pocket flap to each back leg, 2¾ in. (7 cm) down from the raw edge of the waistline and centered on the width (see page 117). Sew buttons to the pant leg to finish. Put the two remaining pocket flaps to one side.

5 With right sides facing, lay the pant fronts on the backs and machine stitch the side seams together, inserting a folded 1½-in. (4-cm) strip of contrast tape into one of the sides to create a decorative tab. Press the seam allowances toward the back leg and topstitch the side seams through all thicknesses.

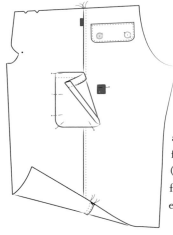

6 Lay a pocket bag on top of one front/back leg section, 9½ in. (24 cm) down from the raw edge of the waistline and with the left-hand edge 3 in. (8 cm) from the side seam. Insert a folded 1½-in. (4-cm) strip of contrast tape into the side for the pocket tab and topstitch close to the edges of the pocket.

7 Attach a pocket flap ⅜ in. (1 cm) above each pocket bag (see page 117). Sew buttons to the pocket bag to finish. Repeat steps 6–7 to make the pocket for the other front/back leg section.

8 With right sides together, fold one front section of the pants on the back section and machine stitch the inner leg seam. Press the seam open. Repeat for the other leg.

9 Turn one leg right side out and pull it into the other leg, so that the right sides are facing. With raw edges aligned, pin, baste (tack), and machine stitch along the curved center seam from the back top edge to the fly front point marked on the pattern piece. Trim the seam allowance on the curve.

10 Make a fake fly front (see page 116).

11 Turn the pants right side out and add two short bars of dense zigzag stitches in contrasting color of thread to the fly front topstitching. Make a decorative buttonhole in a contrasting color of thread through all thicknesses of the fly front, 1¼ in. (3 cm) in from the raw edge of the waistline (do not cut open). Make a loop from a 4-in. (10-cm) length of bias binding, and attach it to the waistband edge.

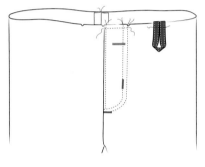

12 Assemble and attach the waistband, thread through the elastic, and hand stitch the opening in the waistband closed (see page 116).

13 On each pant leg, press hem ¾ in. (2 cm) to the wrong side and machine stitch in place. Sew a button on top of the decorative flyfront buttonhole to finish.

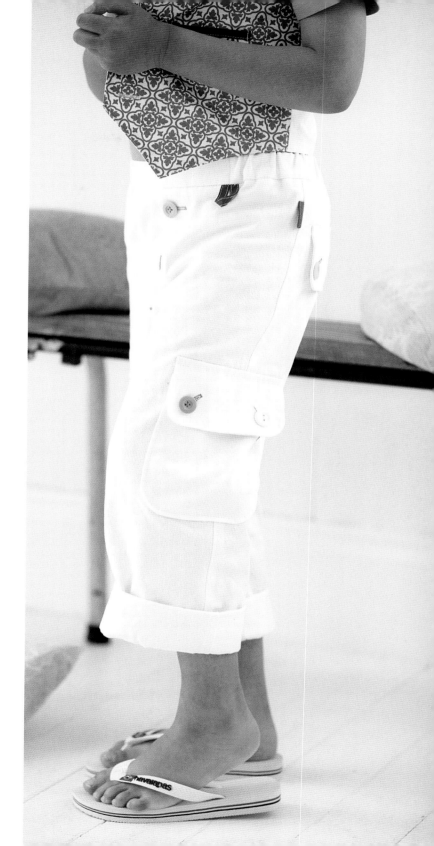

Techniques

Patterns and templates

TRANSFERRING PATTERNS AND TEMPLATES
The patterns that you need to make the projects in this book are on pull-out sheets at the back. They are all full size, so you do not need to enlarge them. Following the required size, trace the patterns you need, including all markings, onto tissue paper, tracing paper, or pattern paper, and cut them out, cutting along the required line; unless otherwise stated in an individual project, a 3/8-in. (1-cm) seam allowance (stitching line) is included but not printed on the patterns.

Appliqué motifs and shaped pockets for the garments are given as trace-off templates on pages 120–125. Trace any templates that you need, including all markings, onto thin card. Place them on the wrong side of the fabric and draw around them, using either tailor's chalk or a fade-away fabric marker pen.

BALANCE MARKS
Short, straight lines at the edges of the pattern indicate points that need to be matched across different pattern pieces. Transfer them from the paper pattern to the fabric, using tailor's chalk or a fade-away fabric marker pen. Alternatively, snip the fabric edges, making balance mark "notches." It's also a good idea to notch the end of fold lines and center lines.

POSITIONAL MARKS
Dots on patterns also indicate points that need to be matched, as well as the position of pockets, buttons, eyelets, and so on, and any areas that require embellishment with embroidery stitches. After cutting, transfer all markings to the wrong side of the fabric before removing the paper pattern, using pins, tailor's chalk, or a fade-away fabric marker pen.

General techniques

CUTTING OUT FABRIC
Lay your fabric on a flat surface and smooth it out. To cut one fabric piece, place the paper pattern on single-thickness fabric, right side up.

To cut "mirror image" left and right fabric pieces, place the paper pattern on double-thickness fabric, folding the fabric with right sides together.

To cut one symmetrical fabric piece from a half paper pattern, place the straight, solid outer line of the paper pattern on the fold of the double-thickness fabric, folding the fabric with right sides together. Pin the paper pattern pieces to the fabric and cut along the edge, using sharp fabric scissors.

REINFORCING WITH FUSIBLE INTERFACING
Interfacing is used to reinforce and stiffen areas such as collars, shoulder straps, pocket flaps, and waistbands. Fusible (iron-on) interfacings, which have heat-sensitive glue on one side, are the easiest to use. Lay the cut interfacing pieces adhesive side down on the wrong side of the garment pieces and, using your iron, follow the manufacturer's instructions to apply. Check that the interfacing is fused all over and re-press any loose areas.

STAY STITCHING
This is a small machine stitch sewn into the seam allowance of a curved edge, approximately 1/8 in. (5 mm) in from the permanent line of stitching, to keep the curve from stretching or distorting.

DOUBLE HEMMING

Depending on the measurements given in each project, fold the edge of the fabric over to the wrong side and press. Fold over again, pin, baste (tack), press, and machine stitch in place, stitching as close as possible to the folded edge.

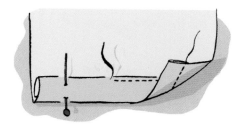

SHORTENING A ZIPPER FASTENER

1 Measure the length of the opening to be fitted with the zipper fastener and mark this length on the zipper tape. Open the zipper and cut the zipper tapes below the stoppers.

2 For nylon zippers, carefully trim off the teeth above the markings, fold under the trimmed zipper tapes, and sew a small bar on each zipper tape over the first tooth with buttonhole thread.

3 For metal zippers, remove the stoppers from the zipper tape and retain. Remove the metal teeth above the markings with pliers and re-attach the stoppers above the remaining teeth.

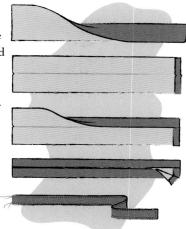

MAKING WAIST AND SHOULDER TIES AND DRAWSTRINGS

METHOD 1

Refer to the individual project instructions for the sizes of the pieces; you need two pieces for each tie or drawstring. With right sides together and aligning the edges, pin, baste (tack), and machine stitch the pieces together in pairs, leaving the short, straight ends open. Trim ¼ in. (5 mm) from the raw edges and cut out little wedges around the tip. Turn right side out and press.

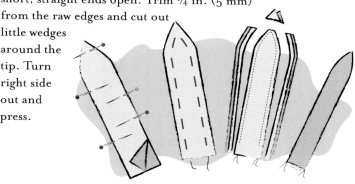

METHOD 2

Refer to the individual project instructions for the sizes of the pieces; you need one piece for each tie or drawstring. Fold one strip in half widthwise and press. Open out, fold in ⅜ in. (1 cm) at one short end, and press. Fold both long raw edges in to the center crease line and press. Fold in half again along the center crease line, and topstitch as close as possible along both long edges and the folded short end.

GATHERING BY HAND

With a needle and thread, work running stitches along the edge to be gathered. Knot one end of the thread and gently pull the other end to gather the fabric to the required length, making sure the gathers are even. Secure with a few stitches at the end.

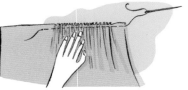

GATHERING BY MACHINE

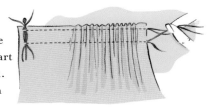

Using the longest stitch length, machine stitch two parallel lines 3/8 in. (1 cm) apart along the edge to be gathered, one 1/4 in. (5 mm) and the other 5/8 in. (1.5 cm) in from the edge. Secure all the threads at one end with a pin and gently pull the two top threads at the other end to gather the fabric to the required length, making sure the gathers are even. Secure these threads with another pin. When attaching the gathered fabric to another fabric piece, use a normal stitch length and machine stitch between the parallel lines of stitching to secure. Remove the parallel lines of stitching to finish.

MAKING A RUFFLED HEM

Double hem or "picot" the raw edge of the fabric before starting. Lay the piece of fabric to be gathered wrong side up on your work surface. Pin one end of a length of elastic (refer to the individual project for the length) to one side edge of the fabric. Using your sewing machine, insert the needle into both the elastic and fabric at one end. Sew a few machine stitches to hold the elastic in place. Holding one end of the fabric securely with one hand, pull the other end with your other hand, so that the elastic stretches to the same width as the fabric. Carefully stitch through all thicknesses, ensuring the elastic is running parallel to the edge of the fabric and the fabric itself is lying as flat as possible beneath.

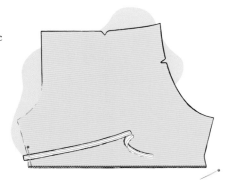

SETTING IN A SLEEVE

1 Using the longest machine stitch, sew 3/8 in. (1 cm) inside and around the sleeve head between the balance marks (notches). With right sides facing, machine stitch the sleeve together at the underarm seam and press open.

2 With right sides together, pin the sleeve edge to the armhole edge, matching the underarm seams, sleeve/armhole notches, the center dot on the sleeve head with the shoulder seam, and the remaining two dots.

3 Pull the easing stitches so that the sleeve gently gathers up and fits the armhole, remembering to distribute the fullness evenly. Pin, baste (tack), and machine stitch the sleeve in place. Remove the easing stitches and shrink out the fullness with a steam iron.

ATTACHING A SHIRT COLLAR

It is essential that all balance marks (notches) and dots on patterns are transferred to their corresponding fabric pattern pieces.

1 Attach fusible (iron-on) interfacing to the wrong side of the top collar, machine stitch 3/8 in. (1 cm) in from the notched edge, fold under, and press.

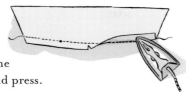

2 With right sides facing, stitch the top collar to the collar facing (under collar), leaving the notched edges open. Trim the seam allowance and snip off the corners. Turn the collar right side out and press.

3 Snip the neck edge of the garment to the stay stitching. With right sides together and aligning the raw edges, pin the collar facing (under collar) to the neck edge of the garment, matching the notches, placing the ends of the collar at the center front of the garment and the dots at the shoulder seams. Machine stitch the collar to the neck edge.

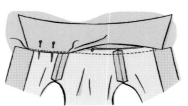

4 Trim the seam allowance, snip the curves, and press the seam allowance toward the inside of the collar. Hand or machine stitch the pressed edge of the top collar over the neck seam.

ATTACHING A COAT COLLAR

It is essential that all balance marks (notches) and dots on patterns are transferred to their corresponding fabric pattern pieces.

1 Attach fusible (iron-on) interfacing to the wrong side of the top collar and machine stitch 3/8 in. (1 cm) in from the notched edge. Snip the notched edge to the machine stitching at the dots and press the seam allowance between the snips, as illustrated.

2 With right sides facing, stitch the top collar to the collar facing (under collar), leaving the notched edges open. Trim the seam allowance, snip off the corners, turn the collar right side out, and press.

3 With right sides together and aligning the raw edges, pin the collar facing (under collar) to the neck edge of the garment, matching the notches and placing the dots at the shoulder seams. Machine stitch both top collar and facing to the front neck edge as far as the folded-under/pressed edge.

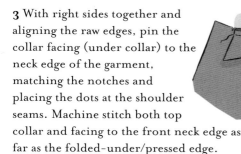

4 Machine stitch the collar facing (under collar) section only to the remaining section of the neck edge. Once the front facings of the garment have been attached (refer to each individual project), carefully stitch the pressed edge of the top collar over the neck seam.

MAKING A FAKE FLY FRONT

1 Turn one leg right side out and pull it into the other leg, so that the right sides are facing. With raw edges aligned, pin, baste (tack), and machine stitch along the curved center seam from the back top edge to the fly front point marked on the pattern piece. Trim the seam allowance on the curve.

2 Fold one fly front extension to the inside along the center front line, press the fold, and edge stitch.

3 With right sides facing, lay the outer fly front extension on top of the inner fly front extension and secure with machine stitches at the upper edges.

4 Using the curved outer edge of the fly extension as a stitching guide, machine stitch the extensions together through all thicknesses.

MAKING AN ELASTICATED WAIST CASING

Double hem the top edge of the garment by folding under ¼ in. (5 mm) and then ¾ in. (2 cm) to the wrong side, and press. Pin, baste (tack), and edge stitch the casing in place, leaving a gap in the stitching to insert the elastic. Thread elastic (refer to the individual project instructions for the length) through the casing, adjusting it to fit the waist comfortably. Sew the ends of the elastic together and stitch the opening closed.

MAKING AND ATTACHING AN ELASTICATED WAISTBAND

1 Before assembling the waistband, make sure all balance marks (notches) are snipped into the fabric piece. With right sides together, machine stitch the short ends of the waistband together to form a loop. Press open the seam. With wrong sides together, fold the loop in half lengthwise and press in a crease; this will be the top edge of the waistband. Open out, fold under ⅜ in. (1 cm) in from one edge, and press.

2 With right sides facing, pin, baste (tack), and machine stitch the waistband to the upper edge of the pants, matching the center front and side seam notches and the seam of the waistband with the center front, side seams, and center back seam of the pants.

3 Turn the waistband to the inside. Pin, baste (tack), and edge stitch the waistband in place, leaving a gap in the stitching along the interfaced area.

4 Thread elastic through the waistband, adjusting it to fit the waist comfortably. Secure both ends of the elastic by sewing a vertical row of machine stitches through all thicknesses of the waistband at each end of the interfaced area.

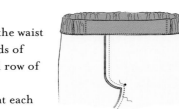

5 Stitch the open flat area of the waistband closed.

MAKING A PATCH POCKET

Fold under one edge of a fabric square (refer to each individual project for details of the size). Press in the fold and machine stitch through all thicknesses. Aligning the top edges, place the pocket template on the fabric square and wrap the excess fabric over it, steam pressing flat as you go around the template. Remove the template and trim down the excess to 3/8 in. (1 cm).

MAKING A TWO-PIECE POCKET OR MARTINGALE

Pin the pieces right sides together and carefully sew around the edges, leaving a gap in the stitching at one side in order to turn the pocket/martingale right side out. Remove the pins and carefully cut around the edges leaving a narrow seam allowance. Turn the pocket/martingale right side out, neaten the side edge by tucking in the seam allowance, and press. Topstitch close to the edge of the pocket/martingale to attach it to the garment.

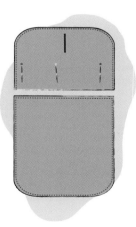

MAKING AND ATTACHING A POCKET FLAP

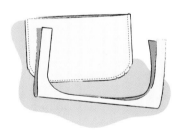

1 Fold the fabric in half, right sides together. Lay the pocket flap template on the folded fabric, aligning the straight edge of the template with the two raw edges, and draw around the template. Smooth the doubled fabric free of wrinkles, pin the layers together, and carefully machine stitch along the drawn line.

2 Remove the pins and carefully cut around the edges, leaving a narrow seam allowance.

3 Turn the pocket flap right side out, press, topstitch around the edges, and work a buttonhole. Place the long, straight edge of the pocket flap 3/8 in. (1 cm) above the patch pocket, right side down, and stitch in place. Trim down the seam allowance, fold the flap back on itself, press, and machine stitch along the top edge of the flap through all thicknesses.

Decorative effects

BIAS BINDING

Fold a length of ready-made bias binding over lengthwise, gently steam-pressing as you fold. Neatly insert the raw edge of the fabric to be bound into the folded binding. Pin, baste (tack), and machine stitch in place. Note: "Shrink" the binding around curves with a steam iron before machine sewing to avoid puckering.

To make your own binding, cut a length of fabric 2 in. (5 cm) wide on the bias—at an angle of 45° to the selvage (self-finished edge of fabric). Fold both long edges over to the wrong side so that they meet in the exact center of the strip. Steam press the folds. Aligning the folded edges, re-fold the strip in half, and press. Attach in the same way as for ready-made bias binding.

PICOT EDGING

Fold the raw edge of the fabric over to the wrong side by 3/8 in. (I cm), or as stated. Steam press in a crisp fold. Machine stitch along the edge, using small zigzag stitches, guiding the needle of your sewing machine so that it falls off the fabric, wrapping the threads around the edge. Carefully trim away the seam allowance, taking extra care not to cut the thread.

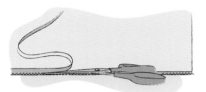

APPLIQUÉ

Trace the appliqué motif onto thin card and cut out. Cut a square of paper-backed fusible bonding web large enough to accommodate the appliqué motif. Lay the square on the wrong side of your appliqué fabric, adhesive side down, and press with a hot iron to heat bond.

I Place the card template on the paper-backed side of the appliqué fabric and draw around it with a pencil. Carefully cut out the motif and peel away the paper backing.

2 Place the motif, adhesive side down, on the main fabric and press with a hot iron to attach. For a professional finish, machine stitch all around the motif with a small, dense zigzag stitch.

MAKING A TAILORED BOW

Cut a length of your chosen fabric or trim (refer to the individual project instructions for the length) and zigzag stitch the short ends together to make a loop. Stitch along the center of the loop, through both layers, to secure.

Cut a shorter length of the same fabric or trim and wrap it around the middle of the loop, securing it with a few stitches at the back. Lay the bow on top of the garment and stitch it in place.

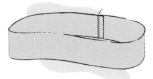

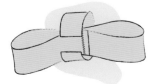

BACKSTITCH

Work from right to left. Bring the needle up at A, down at B, and up again at C. The distance between A and B should be the same as the distance between A and C. To begin the next stitch, insert the needle at A again.

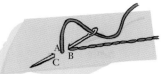

FRENCH KNOT

Bring the needle up from the back of the fabric to the front. Wrap the thread two or three times around the tip of the needle. Reinsert the needle at the point where it first emerged, holding the wrapped threads with the thumbnail of your non-stitching hand, and pull the needle through.

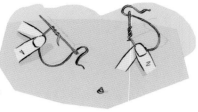

The perfect finish

PRESSING SEAMS

Press seams open from the wrong side, unless instructed otherwise. (If you press seams from the right side, you may mark the fabric.) If you are stitching together two pieces that already have seams, press open the first seams, snip off the corners of the seam allowances, and align the seams exactly (if appropriate) when pinning the fabric pieces together.

TRIMMING SEAM ALLOWANCES

To get the best possible shape to collars, cuffs, and waistbands, carefully trim down the seam allowances to about $\frac{1}{4}$ in. (5 mm) after stitching.

SNIPPING CORNERS

Snip diagonally across the seam allowance at corners to eliminate bulk and to achieve neat right angles when the garment is turned right side out.

FINISHING CURVED EDGES

On curved seams, it is important to clip into the seam allowance after stitching to maintain smooth curves when the garment is turned right side out and the seam allowances are pressed flat. For inward curves, cut small slits. For outward curves, cut wedge-shaped notches.

USING PINKING SHEARS

Using the saw-toothed blades of pinking shears to trim down seam allowances after stitching not only minimizes the risk of the seam allowances fraying, but also provides the notches required for smooth curved seams.

FINISHING CUT EDGES

Use the zigzag stitch on your sewing machine—using the maximum stitch width and length—to neaten hems and seam edges and minimize fraying. Alternatively, for a truly professional finish, use a serger/overlocking machine, which simultaneously trims and over-edge stitches a raw/cut edge.

Templates

LITTLE MISS MARGUERITE
(PAGE 94)
TREE
Enlarge by 200%

LITTLE MISS MARGUERITE
(PAGE 94)
DAISY
Enlarge by 200%

SPOT ON (PAGE 36)
BOW
Enlarge by 200%

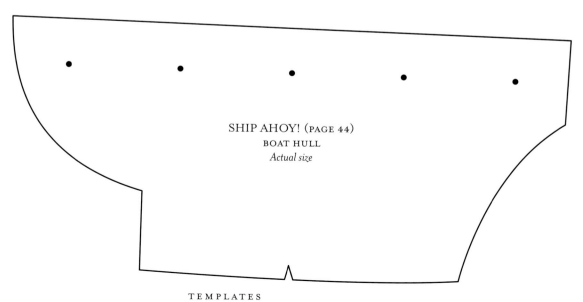

SHIP AHOY! (PAGE 44)
BOAT HULL
Actual size

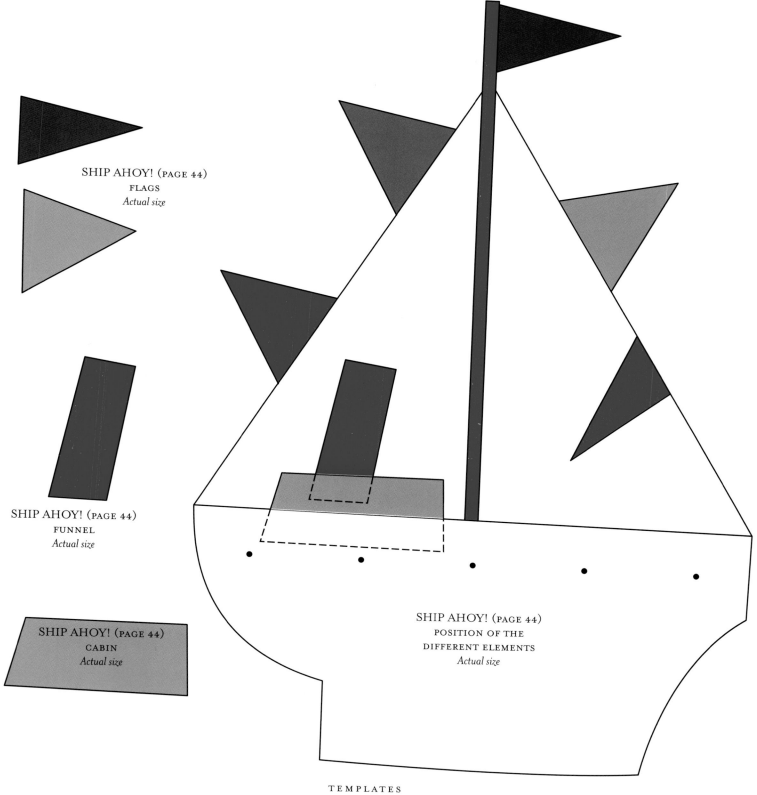

SHIP AHOY! (PAGE 44)
FLAGS
Actual size

SHIP AHOY! (PAGE 44)
FUNNEL
Actual size

SHIP AHOY! (PAGE 44)
CABIN
Actual size

SHIP AHOY! (PAGE 44)
POSITION OF THE
DIFFERENT ELEMENTS
Actual size

LITTLE MONSTER (PAGE 9)
SKULL
Enlarge by 200%

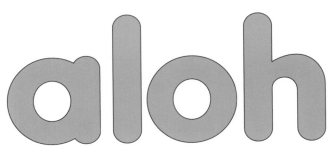

HAWAIIAN TROPICAL (PAGE 39)
LETTERING
Enlarge by 200%

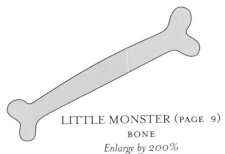

LITTLE MONSTER (PAGE 9)
BONE
Enlarge by 200%

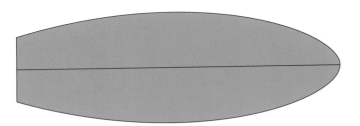

HAWAIIAN TROPICAL (PAGE 39)
SURFBOARD
Enlarge by 200%

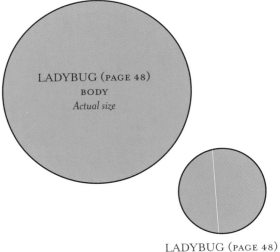

LADYBUG (PAGE 48)
BODY
Actual size

LADYBUG (PAGE 48)
HEAD
Actual size

LADYBUG (PAGE 48)
ANTENNA
Actual size

LADYBUG (PAGE 48)
WINGS
Actual size

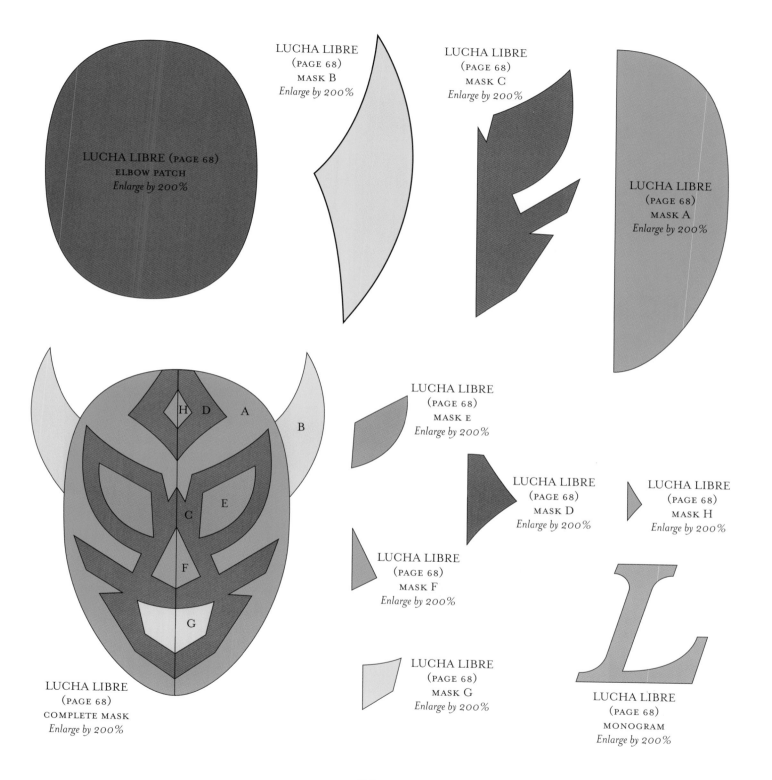

LUCHA LIBRE (PAGE 68)
ELBOW PATCH
Enlarge by 200%

LUCHA LIBRE
(PAGE 68)
MASK B
Enlarge by 200%

LUCHA LIBRE
(PAGE 68)
MASK C
Enlarge by 200%

LUCHA LIBRE
(PAGE 68)
MASK A
Enlarge by 200%

LUCHA LIBRE
(PAGE 68)
MASK E
Enlarge by 200%

LUCHA LIBRE
(PAGE 68)
MASK D
Enlarge by 200%

LUCHA LIBRE
(PAGE 68)
MASK H
Enlarge by 200%

LUCHA LIBRE
(PAGE 68)
MASK F
Enlarge by 200%

LUCHA LIBRE
(PAGE 68)
COMPLETE MASK
Enlarge by 200%

LUCHA LIBRE
(PAGE 68)
MASK G
Enlarge by 200%

LUCHA LIBRE
(PAGE 68)
MONOGRAM
Enlarge by 200%

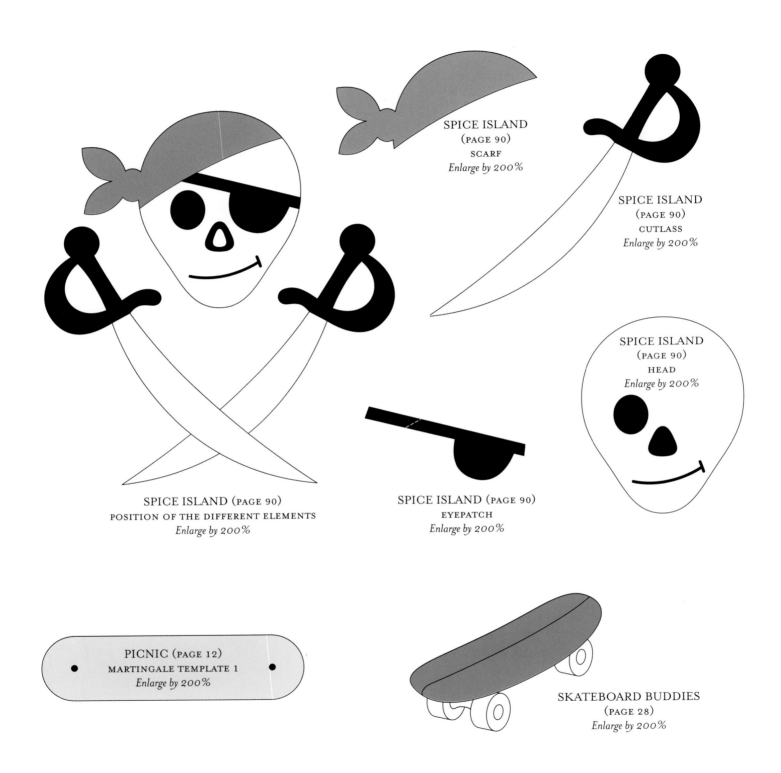

SPICE ISLAND
(PAGE 90)
SCARF
Enlarge by 200%

SPICE ISLAND
(PAGE 90)
CUTLASS
Enlarge by 200%

SPICE ISLAND
(PAGE 90)
HEAD
Enlarge by 200%

SPICE ISLAND (PAGE 90)
POSITION OF THE DIFFERENT ELEMENTS
Enlarge by 200%

SPICE ISLAND (PAGE 90)
EYEPATCH
Enlarge by 200%

PICNIC (PAGE 12)
MARTINGALE TEMPLATE 1
Enlarge by 200%

SKATEBOARD BUDDIES
(PAGE 28)
Enlarge by 200%

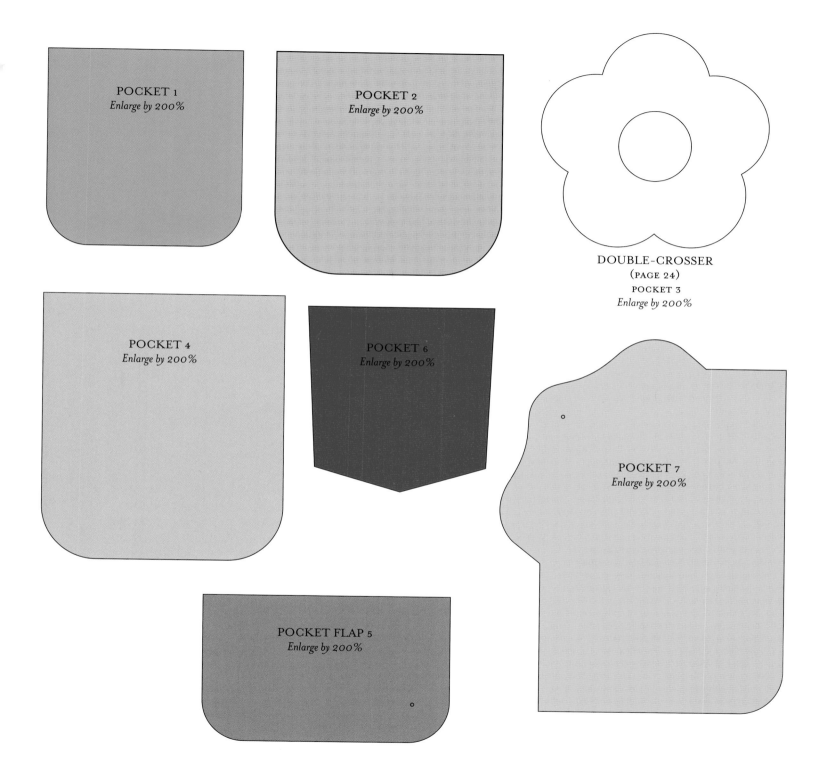

POCKET 1
Enlarge by 200%

POCKET 2
Enlarge by 200%

DOUBLE-CROSSER
(PAGE 24)
POCKET 3
Enlarge by 200%

POCKET 4
Enlarge by 200%

POCKET 6
Enlarge by 200%

POCKET 7
Enlarge by 200%

POCKET FLAP 5
Enlarge by 200%

suppliers

US Suppliers

A.C. Moore
Stores nationwide
1-888-226-6673
www.acmoore.com

Britex Fabrics
146 Geary Street
San Francisco
CA 94108
415–392–2910
www.britexfabrics.com

Cia's Palette
4155 Grand Ave S.
Minneapolis
MN 55409
612–823–5558
www.ciaspalette.com

Hobby Lobby
Stores nationwide
www.hobbylobby.com

Jo-Ann Craft Store
Stores nationwide
1-888-739-4120
www.joann.com

Michaels
Stores nationwide
1-800-642-4235
www.michaels.com

Purl Soho
459 Broome Street
New York
NY 10013
212–420–8796
www.purlsoho.com

Reprodepot Fabrics
413–527–4047
www.reprodepot.com

Tinsel Trading Company
1 West 37th Street
New York
NY 10018
212–730–1030
www.tinseltrading.com

Z and S Fabrics
681 S. Muddy Creek Road
Denver
PA 17517
www.zandsfabrics.com

UK Suppliers

Borovick Fabrics Ltd
16 Berwick Street
London W1F 0HP
020 7437 2180
www.borovickfabricsltd.co.uk

The Cloth House
47 Berwick Street
London W1F 8SJ
020 7437 5155
www.clothhouse.com

Duttons for Buttons
Oxford Street
Harrogate
North Yorkshire HG1 1QE
01423 502 092
www.duttonsforbuttons.co.uk

Dreamtime
6 Pierrepoint Row
Camden Passage
London N1 8EF

Kleins
5 Noel Street
London W1F 8GD
020 7437 6162
www.kleins.co.uk

Liberty
Regent Street
London W1B 5AH
020 7734 1234
www.liberty.co.uk

MacCulloch & Wallis
25–26 Dering Street
London W15 1AT
020 7629 0311
www.macculloch-wallis.co.uk

VV Rouleaux
102 Marylebone Lane
London W1U 2QD
020 7224 5179
www.vvrouleaux.com

European Suppliers

Almacenes Cobian
2 Plaza Pontejos
28012 Madrid
00 34 91 522 25 25
www.almacenescobian.es

Les Coupons de Saint-Pierre
1 place de Saint-Pierre
75018 Paris
00 33 1 42 52 10 79
www.les-coupons-de-saint-pierre.fr

La Droguerie
9–11 rue du Jour
75001 Paris
00 33 1 45 08 93 27
www.ladroguerie.com

Entrée des Fournisseurs
8 rue des Francs Bourgeois
75003 Paris
00 33 1 48 87 58 98
www.entreedesfournisseurs.fr

Megino
12 Calle Corredera Alta
de San Pablo
28004 Madrid
00 34 91 522 64 50
www.megino.net

Le Rouvray
6 rue des Grands Dégres
75005 Paris
00 33 1 43 25 00 45
www.lerouvray.com

Tissus Reine
3–5 place Saint-Pierre
75018 Paris
00 33 1 46 06 02 31
www.tissus-reine.com

Les Touristes
17 rue des Blancs-Manteaux
75004 Paris
00 33 1 42 72 10 84
www.lestouristes.eu

index

Average size chart

Age	Chest	Waist	Height	
3 months	18½ in. (47 cm)	17¼ in. (44 cm)	24½ in. (62 cm)	⎫
6 months	19¼ in. (49 cm)	18 in. (46 cm)	26¾ in. (68 cm)	⎬ INFANT
9 months	20 in. (51 cm)	18¾ in. (48 cm)	29 in. (74 cm)	⎭
1 year	20¾ in. (53 cm)	19¾ in. (50 cm)	31¼ in. (80 cm)	⎫ TODDLER
2 years	22 in. (56 cm)	20½ in. (52 cm)	36¼ in. (92 cm)	⎭
3 years	22½ in. (57 cm)	20¾ in. (53 cm)	38½ in. (98 cm)	⎫
4 years	22¾ in. (58 cm)	21¼ in. (54 cm)	41 in. (104 cm)	⎬ CHILD
5 years	23¼ in. (59 cm)	21¾ in. (55 cm)	43¼ in. (110 cm)	⎭

PROJECT INSTRUCTIONS AND PULL-OUT PATTERNS

The patterns in the pull-out section are full size, so you do not need to enlarge them. Copy them onto tracing paper or dressmaker's pattern paper and then cut them out; that way, they can be reused again and again.

Each pattern is designed for three different ages. On the project pages, the fabric amounts are for the age given in bold type; slight adjustments will be necessary if you are making the project for one of the other sizes. The key on the patterns shows which lines you need to follow. Seam allowances are included where applicable; check the text for each project, as some measurements may vary.

Some of the patterns are shown as halves. When you come to cut out these pieces of fabric, fold the material in half and align the CENTER FOLD LINE on the pattern with the fold in the fabric.

Where there are left and right sides to a garment piece—for example, the left and right front of a shirt—cut one side, then flip the pattern over before you pin it to the fabric and cut the second side.

Measurements in the instructions are given in both imperial and metric. Follow one set of measurements only; do not mix the two.